TIMPSON'S
COUNTRY CHURCHES

TIMPSON'S
COUNTRY CHURCHES

WEIDENFELD & NICOLSON

First published in Great Britain in 1998 by
Weidenfeld & Nicolson

Text copyright © John Timpson, 1998
Photographs copyright © Christoper Dalton,
1998

A CIP catalogue record for this book is available
from the British Library.

ISBN 0 297 823884

Designed by Nigel Soper
Printed and Bound in

Endpapers: Bromfield, Shropshire
Title page: Tichborne, Hampshire

Weidenfeld & Nicolson
The Orion Publishing Group
Orion House
5 Upper St Martin's Lane
London WC2H 9EA

FOREWORD

ALL OUR ENGLISH COUNTRY CHURCHES were built as places of worship and praise and prayer, and they have fulfilled that role for many centuries, but the people who built them ranged from simple Saxon missionaries to empire-building Norman priors, from wealthy Tudor merchants wanting to impress the neighbours to self-indulgent Georgian squires who just wanted to improve their view. They added their individual touches, and so did their architects and craftsmen – people who could make mistakes, who could indulge their own eccentricities, and who quite often had a lively sense of humour.

Subsequent generations made their own additions and changes, often with unexpected results. In particular, rich Victorian 'squarsons' who had never heard of the word 'faculty' sometimes transformed the appearance of their churches, not always for the better, and left us with even more to marvel at, or chuckle over, or blink at in disbelief.

The late Sir John Betjeman, doyen of country church enthusiasts, once wrote that they all possessed a treasure of some sort, 'in wood, stone, iron, tile or glass'. He was referring primarily to Norfolk churches, but it applies to all the churches in this book, though the type of treasure may not be exactly what Sir John had in mind.

As a start he quoted 'wooden angels in their high-up roofs'. I would agree with him on that, if they turn out to be carved on old bed-heads, like the ones I found in a church roof in Suffolk, but I prefer the more unexpected roof decorations, like the papier-mâché elephants in a church in Berkshire, or the sow with her litter of pigs on a boss in Devon, which played a significant role in the foundation of the church. I have included, however, a traditional angel from a little church in Cornwall, because it has the distinction of being dedicated to Sir John himself.

Next on his list of treasures were box pews, bench ends and stained glass. I confess I am not too excited about box pews, although I did find some delightful ones in

Cumbria with numbers on the doors to make them look like compartments in an early railway carriage. Bench ends can be much more entertaining, especially the ones carved by medieval jokers to depict the Seven Deadly Sins. And among the standard biblical scenes in Victorian stained-glass windows it was refreshing to find the Madonna in Nottinghamshire who is holding two babies, one white, one black. I also had to look twice at a traditional 'Suffer the little children' window in Cambridgeshire, in which everyone wears biblical costume but one small boy – in whose memory it is – has a modern face straight from the family album.

Sir John's other country church treasure was painted screens, and here indeed is where Norfolk scores in my book too, though perhaps for different reasons. I would pick the only one I know which features St Uncumber, the lady saint who grew a beard to avoid being encumbered with a husband. Another shows St Matthew wearing an incongruous pair of glasses, and there is one with a medieval inscription written half in Latin and half in broad Norfolk.

There are all manner of delightful surprises to be found like these, on even the most familiar church furnishings. You might think, for instance, that once you have seen a piscina, you have seen them all – just a little stone sink near the altar to pour the surplus water away. But I found one in Oxfordshire which has a tiny effigy of a crusader lolling cross-legged on the edge of it, like a film star beside his swimming pool, complete with a fascinating theory as to why he is there. Stoups by church doors are for water too, but watch out for the ones with chimneys; they are actually medieval ovens for baking the Communion bread. As for fonts, the best-known water receptacle in country churches, there seems no end to the curious forms they can take, from a black basalt bowl in Bedfordshire made by Josiah Wedgwood to an 'en suite' version in Lincolnshire, built into a pillar. The carvings on them range from the Twelve Labours of the Month, an early form of farming almanac, to the Seven Sacraments, including one in Suffolk featuring a dying patient with a medieval chamberpot under his bed.

So far as the actual buildings are concerned, it is not so much the style or the architectural period that I look for; I rather take the view, I am afraid, that a church must be perpendicular, otherwise it would fall down. I prefer the story behind the building, like the church in Herefordshire said to be built by one of the king's knights who assassinated Thomas à Becket, or the one in Hertfordshire which faces west instead of east because it looked better that way from the squire's window, or the 'Dream Church' in Devon with three naves, as seen by the rector in a dream.

Even a straightforward item like a church clock can have its bizarre variations, from one in Lincolnshire which claims to be the largest one-handed clock in the world, to another in Wiltshire (with two hands) which is probably the cheapest: it is made entirely from scrap. There is a clock in Hertfordshire with only three faces, because the farmer on the fourth side of the church did not want his men to waste their time clock-watching, and another in Merseyside which was given an extra face on one side because the existing one could not be seen from the squire's house. And for good measure, there is a clock-face in Derbyshire which has sixty-three minutes.

These are some of the oddities and eccentricities, the marvels and the mysteries which can be found in country churches. As I have said, they are not the most important aspect of these houses of God, but I hope this book may give them an additional interest, both for those who use their own churches regularly but rarely visit others, and for non-churchgoers who may be encouraged to see these churches for themselves, and find they have much more to offer. It was summed up for me by the rector of one church which attracts so many casual visitors that it runs its own tea-room and souvenir shop: 'We hope they may come here as tourists, and leave as pilgrims.'

And if they put a pound or two in the offertory box on the way out, so much the better …

JOHN TIMPSON

CONTENTS

Mansfield

Lincoln

Nottingham

Leicester

Little
Walsingham

Burnham
Norton

Warham

Burnham
Deepdale

Wighton

Knapton

Edgefield

Happisburgh

Terrington
St Clement

Wellingham

Cawston

Winterton-on-Sea

Kings Lynn

Bawburgh

Upton

Leverington

South
Pickenham

Norwich

Helpston

Walpole
St Peter

South
Walsham

Blundeston

Marholm

Upton

Houghton-
on-the-Hill

Castor

Peterborough

Lakenheath

Hinderclay

Huntingfield

Swaffham Prior

Woolpit

Burgate

Badingham

Northampton

Rushbrooke

Hessett

Dennington

Madingley

Cambridge

Framlingham

Cockayne
Hatley

Hadstock

Boulge

Eyke

Cardington

Acton

Ipswich

Marston
Moretaine

Ashwell

Brent Pelham

Lawford

Luton

Furneux Pelham

Little
Braxted

Colchester

North Marston

Ayot
St Lawrence

Tollesbury

Oxford

West
Wycombe

Chelmsford

Bradwell-on-Sea

Fingest

Greensted-
juxta-Ongar

Hambledon

Great
Warley

Southend

London

Minster-
in-Thanet

Biggin Hill

Stoke D'Abernon

Maidstone

Barfrestone

Yalding

Tudeley

Dover

Brooklands

Steyning

Brighton

Portsmouth

Selsey

0   30 Miles

0   50 Kilometres

1.

SOUTH-EAST ENGLAND

&

EAST ANGLIA

THE DENSITY OF LITTLE SQUARE DOTS IN NORFOLK IS rather greater than in any other county in England, and there is a very good reason. I have quoted Sir John Betjeman before, and I make no apology for quoting him again, because he knew a lot more about churches than I shall ever learn. 'Norfolk is one of the great architetural treasure-houses of Europe, because of its medieval churches. Their profusion is their greatness – there are 659 of them. Some are famous throughout Britain, each is different from its neighbour. And lovers of Norfolk churches can never agree which is the best.' That is one reason. There is another, of course: I live in Norfolk myself …

1 mile E of Bedford off the A603

A charred ensign, a brewer's effigy, a vicar's wife in a window – and a big black basalt bowl

IN THE MINDS OF MANY OLDER PEOPLE, Cardington will always be associated with the ill-fated R101 airship, which flew from Cardington on its maiden flight in 1930, and crashed in France with the loss of forty-nine lives. And there is indeed a memorial in St Mary's, together with the charred remains of the ensign which was recovered from the wreckage. There is a photograph of the memorial at Beauvais, where it crashed, and in the churchyard an altar tomb marks the mass grave of those on board, including the Air Minister, Lord Thomson of Cardington.

But there is more in St Mary's than memories of the R101. In particular there are memories of the Whitbreads, the brewing family who were squires and benefactors of Cardington for many years. It was they who were largely responsible for rebuilding the nave and the tower when the old church became dangerous. Above the family vault they also built the chapel which contains the opulent Whitbread memorials.

The first Samuel Whitbread, founder of the brewery, had some notable friends, among them John Howard the prison reformer, who had a house by the church-yard, and Josiah Wedgwood of pottery fame. Both are remembered in St Mary's: Howard has a memorial tablet, Wedgwood has a font. He made it for Samuel Whitbread, and like Samuel's monument he made it big. It is an imposing bowl of black basalt, which at first glance looks more suitable for a large aspidistra or a few gallons of soup; it must have been an awe-some sight for a baby. But Wedgwood shrewdly provided a little basalt pedestal inside the basalt bowl, on which to place a mini-font of silver gilt – thus obviating the risk of the baby drowning.

Wedgwood made three of these basalt fonts for the Whitbreads. One went to America, another is in Essenden Church in Hertfordshire. I hope there was some sort of reciprocation by the Whitbreads – perhaps in the form of best bitter for basalt bowls …

Apart from all this ostentation, there is another memorial in St Mary's which is rather more discreet. Beside a plaque made of Delft tiles, recording the gratitude of the Dutch airmen who were stationed at Cardington during the war, there is a window dedicated to Martha Jackson Hillier, wife of a past vicar of St Mary's. Although it is not mentioned, those who knew her would appreciate that the central panel actually depicts Martha herself.

BELOW The charred ensign from the wreckage of the ill-fated R101; RIGHT The Wedgwood font among the Whitbread monuments.

7 miles E of Sandy off the B1040

Henry's shopping list: choir-stalls from Charleroi, rails from Malines, a screen from Ghent …

WHEN THE REVD HENRY Cockayne Cust arrived as squire and rector in 1806 he found St John's 'in a most lamentable state of neglect'; the last straw was when snow fell on the altar during a service on Christmas Day. So he embarked on a massive restoration programme, and the church was virtually taken apart and put back together again. From the outside, when he had finished in 1830, it looked much the same, but in far better shape. The interior, however, was completely transformed, thanks to the enthusiastic shopping expeditions, at home and abroad, of Henry Cockayne Cust.

His biggest purchase was in a dealer's shop in Charleroi. He picked up the complete set of seventeenth-century carved stalls and medallioned panels which now fill the chancel. The stalls overflow into the nave, where they face each other, collegiate-style. They originated from a ruined abbey at Oignies in Flanders, and they are considered the finest collection of Flemish carved woodwork anywhere in England.

But that was just the start. On another shopping trip to the Continent Henry bought a Communion rail from a church at Malines, again elaborately carved. It was too long to fit all of it into the chancel, so he put the rest along the front of the organ loft. The big folding doors beneath the loft he found in Louvain, the screen shielding his family pew from the congregation came from Ghent, and he acquired a pulpit from a church in Antwerp. The pulpit was sold on to Carlisle Cathedral in 1963 for £500 – one hopes at a healthy profit – but its sounding-board, showing St Andrew, now serves as the front of the lectern.

On his more local expeditions Henry picked up some angels from a church in Biggleswade to put in the roof. He found some rare thirteenth-century stained glass being dumped by a church in Yorkshire, and some of the glass in the east window came from another church in Kent. His only failure, it seems, was in finding an organ. The pipes in the organ loft, elegantly painted and gilded to emulate those which used to be in King's College, Cambridge, are actually just fakes; there is no organ underneath them.

Amidst all this imported woodwork and glass are some fine home-grown monuments and effigies of the Cockaynes and their relatives, all looking terribly English compared with the French saints and scholars on the backs of the choirstalls. Indeed one wonders how these illustrious French Catholics enjoy their English Protestant surroundings. But I imagine they make their presence felt; they must be extremely uncomfortable to lean back on …

LEFT A section of the imported stalls in the chancel: 'the finest collection of Flemish carved woodwork anywhere in England.'

6 miles SW of Bedford on the A421

The devil failed to fly away with the tower – but what happened to the tenth angel?

THERE ARE NEARLY FORTY CHURCHES in Britain with detached towers, and nearly forty different explanations why – generally involving the Devil. St Mary's is no exception. In this case, they say, the Devil stole it from the church and tried to fly off with it, but after about twenty yards he found it was too heavy and dropped it. As it descended he caught his foot on the parapet and lost a toenail, which fell into a nearby field. And the toenail is still pointed out today, a solitary stone jutting out of the earth.

Apart from the fact that the Devil is generally assumed to have hooves rather than toes, the stone has in fact been identified as the remnant of an ancient cross – but that does not entirely kill the story. The rector, the Revd John Greenway, told me that crosses were often erected on pagan sites of worship. That did not mean any direct connection with the Devil or his toes – 'but on the other hand, where you have non-Christian worship there can be spiritual problems of one kind or another …'

The church guidebook discreetly ignores this story, but does concede there is a mystery about the tower. For a start, it is out of alignment with the church, and the

BELOW The damaged effigies of Thomas Snagge and his wife – no way to treat ancestors of the BBC's famous Boat Race commentator.

lower part was built much earlier than the main building. It also has excessively thick walls, and an unexplained opening halfway up one side. It seems in fact to have been a watchtower and a place of refuge, accessible only by ladder, and it was much later adapted as a belltower for the church. A venerable timber hoist, probably used to haul the bells into place, is still inside it.

Inside St Mary's itself there is a splendid Doom painting above the chancel arch, depicting dazed-looking souls emerging from their tombs, en route either for St Peter and the Golden Gate or a monster with the Jaws of Hell. It was whitewashed over at one stage, probably when the rood screen was taken away. It has now been restored, but all that remains of the screen is a fragment hanging on the wall in the north aisle.

The sixteenth-century effigies of Thomas Snagge and his wife have been damaged too. Toes and fingers have been broken off, which is no way to treat a Speaker of the House of Commons, let alone an ancestor of one of the BBC's best-known commentators. And there is one more mystery, the missing angel in the roof. The original ten were hidden away during all this vandalism, and when they were replaced, only nine were found. So far there is no link with the Devil – unless of course, when he couldn't carry the tower, he came back for a more portable souvenir …

RIGHT Did the Devil try to steal the church tower – or was it just built separately as a watch tower in the first place?

4 miles W of High Wycombe, off the A40 and across M40

The over-sized tower 'with eyebrows raised in unresolved surprise'

CHURCH TOWERS ARE GENERALLY higher than the rest of the church – or they wouldn't be towers – but not many are wider as well. The tower of St Bartholomew's is a great chunk of Norman masonry, sixty feet high and nearly twenty feet square, with walls four feet thick – and eight feet wider than the nave. In fact it was probably used as the nave originally, and the present nave was the chancel. Rather incongruously, it was given a twin-gabled roof a couple of centuries later – 'like eyebrows raised in unresolved surprise', as one visiting poet described it.

Somewhere inside it is one lonely bell. The others were probably sold off after the Reformation, but the more entertaining version is that they were lost by an eighteenth-century rector in a wager with his opposite number at nearby Hambleden. It is the sort of story which prompts a knowing smile and a sceptical shake of the head, but it so happens that the same story is told in Hambleden. Two of their church bells, the treble and the smaller Sanctus bell, are said to have been recast from the Fingest bells – 'won, it is said, at cards', according to the guidebook. And that's good enough for me.

St Bartholomew's is fairly short on memorials as well as bells, but the one to Emily Gowland, 'Friend of the Poor', sets something of a precedent. Memorials often take the form of stained-glass windows, but at Fingest the chancel windows had been blocked up completely – so the windows were 're-opened' in memory of Emily.

Sir William Connor – formerly 'Cassandra' of the *Daily Mirror* – lived in Fingest and wrote about St Bartholomew's in a style far removed from his familiar vitriolic prose. 'Look well at this ancient and sturdy citadel of Christianity,' he exhorted, 'for there is none quite like it in all the land.'

Surprisingly for a *Mirror* man, he did not mention a romantic little custom which his picture editor would have loved. It is said to be unlucky if a bridegroom does not lift his bride over the wishing gate in the churchyard after the wedding; indeed, it has been known for the gate to be locked to ensure that he does. But maybe Sir William purposely kept quiet about it – to make sure the *Mirror* would get an exclusive.

BELOW The first test for bridegrooms – lifting their bride over one of the church gatess.

5 miles W of Marlow, off the A4155

The altar that can claim: 'Cardinal Wolsey slept here'

ANY VERY LARGE CHURCH IN A VERY small village is liable to be dubbed a 'mini-cathedral', but it seems particularly appropriate for a church where the last English saint was baptized before the Reformation. St Thomas de Cantilupe was born in Hambleden in 1218, and St Mary's still has the font in which he was christened. It used to have relics of him too, but his bones are buried in a full-size cathedral, the one at Hereford where he was bishop.

The church still has a relic of another notable cleric, however, albeit an unlikely one. The south transept altar is made from Cardinal Wolsey's bed-head – surely the only altar that can claim: 'Cardinal Wolsey slept here.'

The reference books do not make it clear how the bed-head got into the church, or where the bed was when Wolsey slept in it, but the carved panelling incorporates Wolsey's coat of arms, and also that of his colleague, Bishop Fox – though no one has

BELOW Sir Cope D'Oyley and his wife and children. The skulls some of them carry are not just D'Oyley toys …

yet suggested they occupied the bed simultaneously.

The official theory is that it belonged to the Sandys family, whose home near Basingstoke they both used to visit, and when Henry Sandys' widow married Ralph Scrope of Hambleden Manor House, she brought the bed-head with her. It may seem odd for a host to carve his guests' coats of arms on their bed, and odder still for a bride to turn up at her new home with the bed-head from the spare room, but there it now is in St Mary's as part of the Wolsey Altar, and long may such stories survive.

In contrast, the north transept has a more orthodox memorial, displaying the alabaster effigies of Sir Cope D'Oyley and his wife and ten children. The skulls that four of the children carry are not macabre D'Oyley toys; they indicate that they died before their parents. Nearby is a muniment chest belonging to the locally-born seventh Earl of Cardigan, who led the Charge of the Light Brigade – down the wrong valley. And in the upper churchyard is buried another soldier with a rather different reason for being remembered, Major George Howson, who founded the British Legion Poppy Factory and the tradition of wearing poppies on Armistice Day.

Also buried there is W. H. Smith, local squire and retailer of good books, whose chain of bookshops will I hope note this reference and bear it in mind …

RIGHT Part of the Wolsey Altar – the Cardinal's bed-head. Bishop Fox may have used it too, presumably on a different occasion.

6 miles N of Aylesbury off the A413

The rector who put the devil in a boot, and the miserly squire who put the Queen in Balmoral

TWO REMARKABLE CHARACTERS loom large in the history of the church, for very different reasons. One was a fourteenth-century rector with powers of healing, Dr John Schorne, and the other was a nineteenth-century squire with pots of money, John Camden Neild, who went down in history as the Queen's Miser.

Dr Schorne liked to explain his healing powers in a way his congregation could understand, so he used a medieval visual aid. He held up a boot with a small cut-out figure of the Devil, and by a little sleight-of-hand he made the Devil disappear inside the boot, in the way he made disease disappear. Inevitably this led to the story that he could capture the Devil in a boot, and he is depicted on some rood screens giving his demonstration. 'The Devil in a Boot' also features on some inn signs, with the distorted version becoming The Eel's Foot (badly-painted Devils could be mistaken for eels).

After Dr Schorne's death pilgrims poured in to visit his shrine in the church. It became such a money-spinner that the Pope ordered his bones to be transferred to more illustrious surroundings at Windsor. As a slight compensation the Dean of Windsor became the church's patron – and still is. The shrine is marked by a stone cross, and there is a curious hole in the chancel wall, above the vestry, from where the rectors were supposed to be able to watch it, to ensure pilgrims put in a proper contribution – and didn't remove anyone else's. I am reluctant to spoil a good story, but I have looked through that hole, and the shrine is quite out of sight. It would have been more useful for keeping an eye on the chained Bible in the chancel – one of the great treasures of the church.

If John Camden Neild had visited the shrine, his contribution would no doubt have been negligible. Although he had a substantial fortune, he hated spending any of it. When he was approached, as the squire, for help in repairing the church roof, it is said he gave a piece of calico to put over the hole and said, 'That'll see me out …' His memorial tablet in the chancel floor is understandably modest, but he did help the church indirectly. He left all his money to Queen Victoria – about twenty million pounds today. The Queen is said to have spent most of it on buying Balmoral, but she did give the splendid east window in his memory.

I hope there was also a little left over to repair that hole in the roof …

BELOW Dr Schorne's shrine, subsidised by pilgrims. RIGHT Queen Victoria's window, subsidised by the Queen's Miser.

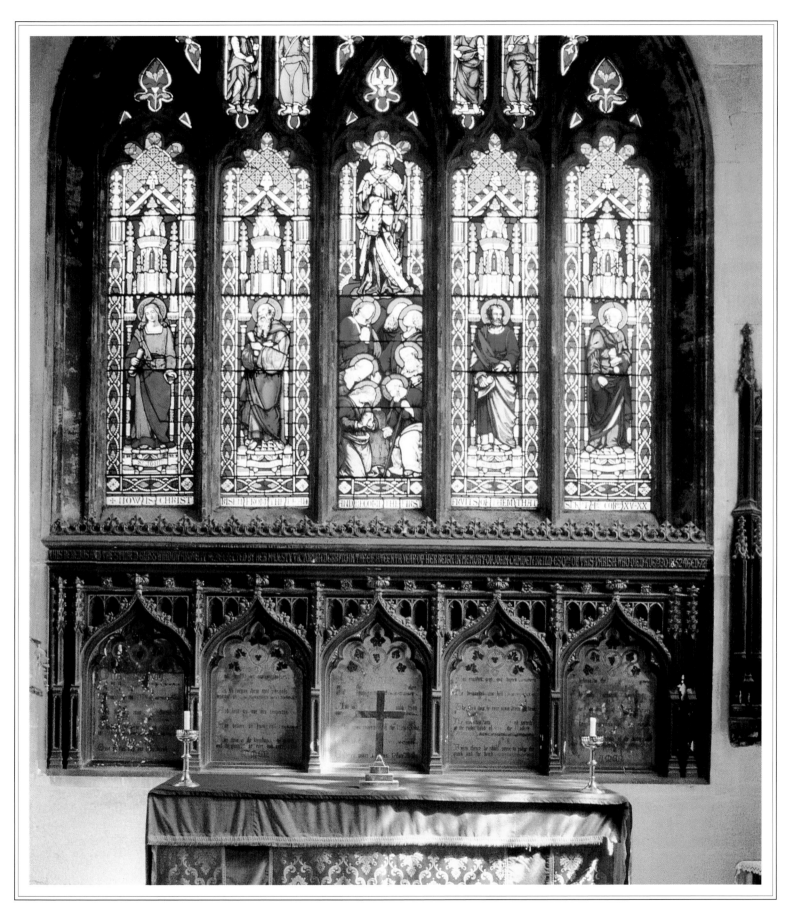

1 mile W of High Wycombe on the A40

Milk punch in the golden ball
– while the doves have a drink in the font

SIR FRANCIS DASHWOOD'S GOLDEN Ball on the tower of St Lawrence's, covered in double gold leaf, is the best-known landmark in the Wycombe Valley. When he rebuilt the church in the eighteenth century he added this final touch to provide a meeting place, so it is said, for members of his famous Hellfire Club – a place where nine could sit in comfort, 'drinking heavenly milk punch and singing bawdy songs unfit for the ears of the worshippers below'.

Actually Sir Francis was a distinguished Cabinet minister, and the Hellfire Club was mainly for top politicians – very appropriately, some might think. It seems more likely that Sir Francis used the Golden Ball for a kind of topping-out ceremony, and he assembled his friends in it after they had admired his new church, to enjoy a celebratory drink.

There is certainly much to admire in St Lawrence's, if you relish this kind of extravagant Italian Baroque. Sir Francis demolished the original nave and built a new one based on the Temple of the Sun at Palmyra, near Damascus. It has sixteen glossy pillars along the walls, and everywhere is decorated with garlands and flowers and doves, from the marble floor to the painted ceiling. There are more doves in the chancel, perhaps looking for a drink, because the rare Italianate font is in the shape of a bird-bath, with four doves permanently perched on it. A serpent, the symbol of evil, is wrapped around the base, but it is just failing to catch the birds as they drink the Water of Life. The babies brought here for bap-

tism must be fascinated by it.

Sir Francis also built the roofless mausoleum beside the church, intended, it is said, for the hearts of his friends – and it did contain at least one. Paul Whitehead, onetime secretary of the Hellfire Club, died in 1775 and bequeathed his heart to Sir Francis – by now Lord le Despencer. It was taken in procession through West Wycombe in a leaden urn, escorted by musicians, soldiers, fifes and muffled drums, and duly installed in the mausoleum. The urn was inscribed: 'Unhallowed hands, this urn forebear'; nevertheless it disappeared in 1829. Happily, Sir Francis's Golden Ball is rather more difficult to shift.

LEFT, BELOW & RIGHT Sir Francis Dashwood's golden ball on top of the tower, the birdbath font complete with birds, and the Italian Baroque entrance to the chancel.

3 miles W of Peterborough off the A47

The saint who was saved by a rolled-up carpet: the non-detachable angels were lucky too

THE MEDIEVAL MASONS WHO REBUILT St Kyneburgha's original Saxon church in 1124 had a considerable advantage: they were virtually building inside a stone quarry, with their materials all around them. Castor was a Roman industrial town, manufacturing clay pottery, and the Roman equivalent of Josiah Wedgwood was able to build himself a vast mansion, covering the same area as Blenheim Palace – the second largest Roman building in Britain. It was abandoned around AD450, and when St Kyneburgha arrived a couple of hundred years later she founded her modest little convent among the ruins. There was still plenty of rubble left when the Normans came, and it went towards building the massive tower which dominates the present church. The spire was added a century or two later, to make it even more imposing.

The masons used some stone from the Saxon church as well, judging by the 'Christ in Majesty' over the main door, which looks like Saxon work. They added their own decorations, particularly on the tower pillars in the church, which have all manner of odd animals doing odd things, watched by some very odd-looking people. There were also two men fighting over a damsel in distress – St Kyneburgha perhaps?

It does not quite fit with her legend which is illustrated on her patronal banner, now protected behind glass – a replica stands by the lectern. There is also a clay model near the site of her shrine, where she lay until her remains were taken to Peterborough Cathedral in the eleventh century. It is said that, while she was out walking, a ruffian attempted to molest her, and as she ran away a carpet of flowers unrolled before her to smooth her path. As she passed over it, the carpet rolled up behind her to form a barrier of thorns, keeping the ruffian at bay.

A medieval wall-painting depicts a more familiar story of a saint under duress, the martyrdom of St Catherine; it shows her being tortured on a wheel, the origin of the Catherine Wheel. But the main theme of the church decorations is angels, whole flights of them with gilded, outstretched wings, poised for take-off in the roof. In the belfry it is possible to reach up and touch one of them, and it becomes clear how so many of the original angels have survived, because it is not a separate carving added to the roof, but actually carved into the roof-beam. If Cromwell's men, or anyone else, had attempted to pull it down, the roof would have come down with it.

LEFT A clay model of St Kyneburgha escaping while a barrier of thorns miraculously unfolds to envelop her pursuer.

5 miles NW of Peterborough, off the A15 on B1443

A peasant poet, a disgruntled mason – and a musical snowball

BOUNDARY CHANGES ARE NO respecters of poets, and Northamptonshire's Peasant Poet, John Clare, is now commemorated in Cambridgeshire. Here in his home village it is difficult to avoid him, particularly if you are heading for the church. On one road to it you pass the plaque on the thatched cottage where he was born, and next to it the Bluebell Inn, where he once worked as a pot-boy and where the John Clare Society meets. On another road you pass the John Clare School, and the two meet at the John Clare Memorial which rather overshadows the ancient Butter Cross on the opposite corner.

Then as you enter the church there is a chunk of stone in the porch inscribed with his name, and just inside is the John Clare Pew, full of memorabilia. In the churchyard round the back is his grave, and if you are in Helpston around his birthday in July you will see the children from the John Clare School processing past the John Clare Memorial to place trays of wild flowers, 'Midsummer Cushions', around the John Clare grave – a village custom recorded, of course, by John Clare.

But St Botolph's has more to offer than memories of a peasant poet, whichever county he belongs to. In particular there are two pieces of stonework in the north aisle, one medieval, the other modern, which demonstrate what a contrast there can be in the stonemason's art. The old one is a 'mason's fool', a roughly carved face with a disgruntled expression, left behind by the mason to express his disgust at what he was paid. I doubt it earned him a pay rise, but I

ABOVE AND LEFT Faces medieval and modern – the 'mason's fool' and the musician.

am sure it made him feel better.

The other is a plaque by the organ, bearing the amazingly lifelike face of Albert Snowball, who came to play the organ for a fortnight and continued as organist for seventy years. It was copied from a photograph taken from the pew alongside him while he was actually playing, and as he peers over his glasses at the music, you can almost hear the opening chords of the next hymn. Services at St Botolph's may never be quite the same for the congregation without seeing Mr Snowball at the organ, but this plaque must be the next best thing.

2 miles NW of Wisbech off the A1101

The lectern went into the stoke-hole, the Jesse into an attic – and the cook went over the spire

THE LOFTY SPIRE OF ST LEONARD'S has been a landmark in this part of the Fens from the early fourteenth century, but the little turrets around its base are something of a mystery. They may be there to strengthen it, or just as a decoration. The locals call them tubs, which is quite a mystery too, but not nearly as mysterious as the fate of a cook who, according to legend, was whirled away over the spire by the Devil when she baked cakes on a Sunday. They still bake 'whirly-cakes' in Leverington, with whirls of chocolate in them – and very delicious they are too – but I am not sure if these are a peace-offering or a defiant gesture. Anyway, nobody has been whirled away lately, so obviously they work …

There must have been a period when church valuables were liable to be whirled away too, perhaps to hide them from vandals, perhaps because their value was not appreciated. The fifteenth-century eagle lectern, for example, with six lions for feet, was rediscovered in 1928 in the stoke-hole.

It was restored and regilded, and is considered to be one of the finest medieval wooden lecterns still surviving in England.

The other rediscovery was the glass from a fifteenth-century Jesse window, this time in the rectory attic. The illustration of Jesse's descendants, down to Jesus, was restored and replaced in the chapel in 1900.

The font was rather more difficult to budge, and remains in its original position. It has saints seated round the bowl, winged angels supporting it, and assorted Christians round the stem. There is also, on one of the steps, 'an incision of unknown significance' – possibly for a book-stand or a candlestick, says the guidebook. Or it may mark an attempt to haul it off to the stoke-hole or the rectory attic.

The east window looks fairly standard, showing Christ raising his hand in blessing over a small boy, with others standing around. They are wearing the usual biblical clothes and have the usual biblical features – but disconcertingly, the small boy's face looks as if it would be more at home in a family photograph album. That indeed may be what it is based on, because it is clearly the face of the son of Mr Peatling of Leverington Hall. Mr Peatling was a great benefactor of the church – it was he who paid for the restoration of the lectern. His son died in childhood, and his father gave the window in his memory.

LEFT The Jesse window: King David is carrying his harp.
RIGHT Spot the modern face of the squire's son in biblical surroundings.

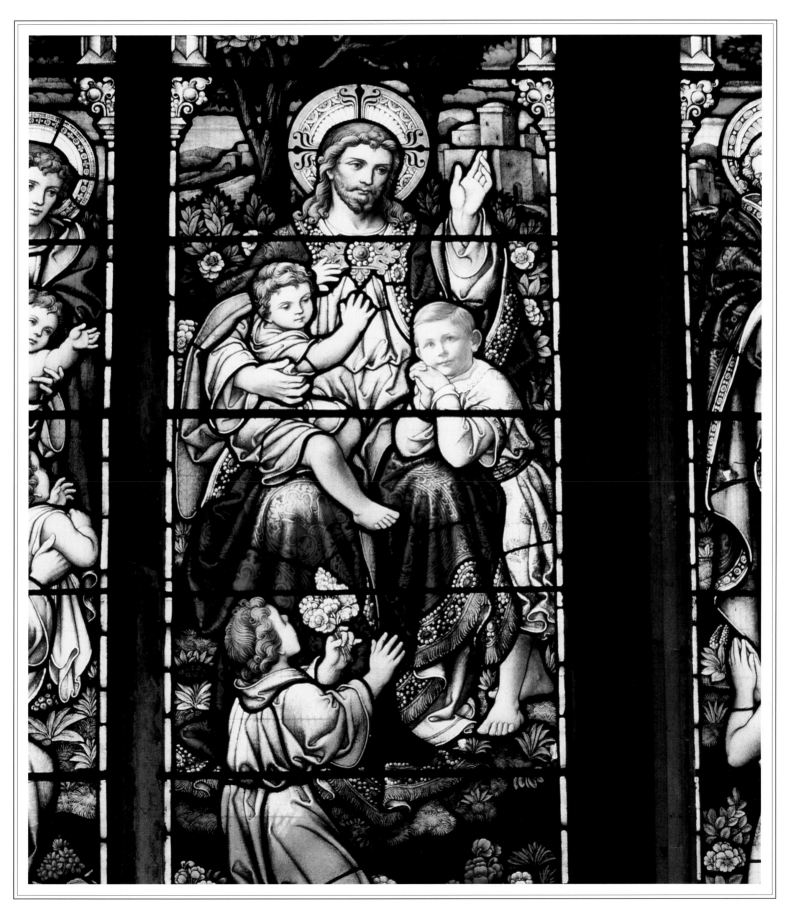

5 miles W of Cambridge off the A45

Squire versus vicar in the case of the altered altar

THE TWO FURNISHINGS FOUND IN every church, the altar and the font, have both been the subject of lively controversy at St Mary's. The altar is a reminder of a bitter feud between the parson and the squire just a hundred years ago, which culminated in a lawsuit at a consistory court.

Mr Hurrell of Madingley Hall strongly objected to the High Church rituals of the vicar, Mr Lacey; he boycotted services and his employees found it wise to stay away too. In 1898, after Mr Lacey had installed a stone altar without a faculty, he saw his chance and took out the lawsuit, and at the end of a long and acrimonious hearing the Chancellor confirmed the altar had to go. Instead, a faculty was granted to the delighted Mr Hurrell to replace it with a wooden one.

The altar was duly removed, but Mr Hurrell took so long to provide a new one that a parishioner called Susan Burnett, perhaps in a spirit of compromise, obtained a fresh faculty – for a wooden altar with a stone block in the centre. It is the one still in use, but perhaps to bury old hatchets it has a close-fitting cover, so no one can tell if it is wood, or stone, or concrete.

Mr Hurrell was also involved in the story of the font, but only indirectly. St Mary's ancient font disappeared a couple of hundred years ago. In 1874 Mr Hurrell demolished part of the Hall and found some stones which had been taken from another church at Histon when the Hall was built – plus a broken font. The font was mended and is now in St Mary's, but is it the original or the one taken from Histon? The experts have argued ever since.

Incidentally, the fourteenth-century bell which is on the floor nearby has an odd history too. It was removed from the belfry in 1926 because they thought it was cracked, but when they got it down they could find nothing wrong. Either they didn't like to admit their mistake or they just couldn't be bothered to haul it up again, so it sits there still.

RIGHT AND OPPOSITE Unlikely neighbours: the church bell and the font, guarding the door.

St Mary's, Marholm

3 miles NW of Peterborough off the A15

A last-ditch defence – ha-ha – for a church where every Fitzwilliam fits

ST MARY'S IS ONE OF MANY LITTLE country churches set in a field, but it has an unusual way of protecting itself from the cattle that share the field with it. Some churches have provided me with a gentle ho-ho, but here for a change is a ha-ha, Capability Brown's method of keeping out livestock without building a wall or planting a hedge to spoil the view, and more commonly found on great estates than around churches. I doubt he invented the name; more likely it was the reaction of the first of his employers who watched his cattle or sheep disappear into it.

Anyway, a ha-ha protects St Mary's, and the only access is across a little footbridge with a sturdy iron gate. It is a useful defence, because there are some great treasures inside, the monuments of the Fitzwilliams spanning four hundred years. They are all in the chancel, which was enlarged in 1530 by the first Fitzwilliam Lord of the Manor, Sir William Fitzwilliam, to ensure each succeeding Fitzwilliam fits.

The monuments illustrate, in one family, how styles have changed over the years. The first Sir William's tomb was sombre,

except for the brasses of a knight and his lady on the back decorated in the Fitzwilliam colours. It was restored a century later – by another Fitzwilliam – but the inscription recording this caused a problem for the craftsman who carved it. One word proved too long for the space he had allocated, so the last letters, much reduced in size, are tucked away on a separate line.

The next, dated 1599, is much grander, with the coloured effigies of another Sir William and his lady lying on an altar tomb, rather touchingly holding hands. A lengthy inscription records how he was appointed by Queen Elizabeth as 'her Lord Lieutenant in Ye Kingdom of Ireland'; one wonders where he went wrong.

The grandest monument is an eighteenth-century Earl Fitzwilliam and his wife Anna, rather larger than life and raised above eye level, looking so enormously dignified it is difficult to picture them holding hands, even in private. And finally there is a comparatively modest and very lifelike, almost homely profile of a twentieth-century Lady Fitzwilliam, bringing the sequence into the present day.

Incidentally, the name of Sir Christopher Wren is also remembered in Marholm Church, but it has nothing to do with his fame as an architect. He happened to marry a Fitzwilliam …

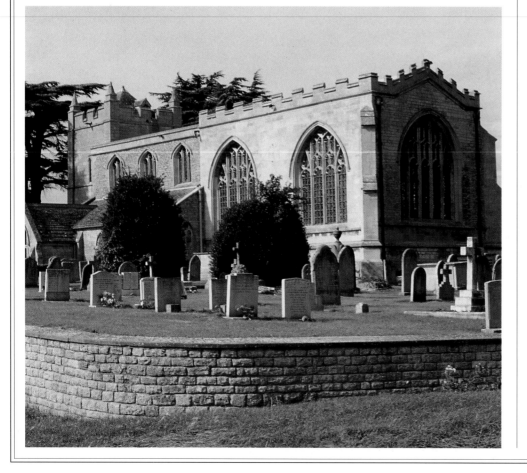

LEFT AND RIGHT The ha-ha around St Mary's, and some of the memorials it helps to protect: contrasting monuments to the Fitzwilliams through the centuries.

7 miles NE of Cambridge on the B1102

One parish, two churches. One was demolished, then the other had problems. And so it went on …

THE FLUCTUATING FORTUNES OF Swaffham Prior's two churches have been linked since 1667, when the two parishes were amalgamated, but they stood side by side on the same site as independent parish churches for four centuries before that. The parish boundary ran through the churchyard; on one side of it the Prior of Ely built St Mary's, on the other, three knights of Count Alan of Brittany built St Cyriac's and St Julitta's. So presumably St Mary's was attended by the locals, and St Cyriac's by the Norman 'incomers' – and it took four hundred years for them to integrate …

When the churches were united the nave of St Cyriac's was demolished and everyone used St Mary's, but a hundred years later St Mary's stone spire was struck by lightning, the parishioners thought the building unsafe, and they decided to rebuild St Cyriac's and use that. But there was a certain lack of forward planning. They began knocking down St Mary's to use the stonework, and reduced it to a ruin before

BELOW Swaffham Prior's two churches (St Mary's on the left)
RIGHT panels in the war memorial windows – 'in appalling taste but fascinating as curios.'

deciding it was impractical, so for some years the village had two ruined churches.

St Cyriac's was completed in the early 1800s, a Georgian church with wooden pillars. It could not have been an ideal design because by the 1870s it had deteriorated so much that the parish decided to go into reverse and move back into the other church. The ruins of St Mary's were restored, and since the turn of the century it has been functioning again as the parish church. St Cyriac's furnishings were removed – St Mary's got some of the windows – and it was left to rot away until 1976, when the Redundant Churches Commission restored it and made it available as a concert hall.

Happily, after this chequered history, St Mary's has prospered. In 1964 the final restoration took place to the unusual tower: it is square at the base, octagonal halfway up and sixteen sided at the top. But the most unusual feature of St Mary's is the 1914–18 War memorial windows, which the guide describes briefly as 'in appalling taste, but fascinating as curios'. They have realistic pictures of battlefields, gun batteries, casualty stations, air battles, even the sinking of the *Lusitania*, and each has an appropriate text. A German plane, for instance, has the line: 'Though they climb up to Heaven, thence will I bring them down'. The 'appalling taste' perhaps refers to the dedication: 'These men died fighting nobly for God, King and Country against the aggression and barbarities of German militarism.' Not exactly in the spirit of peace and goodwill to all men – and these days, certainly not 'politically correct'.

5 miles W of Peterborough, off the A47

The doves above the Doves are logical enough – but can you explain the sundial?

UPTON IS A VERY SMALL ESTATE village, and originally St John's was a very small church. But in 1625 Sir William Dove, son of the Bishop of Peterborough, acquired the estate and decided the church would not be big enough for his family tomb. So he took down the small north aisle and built a new and bigger one, about the same size as the nave itself. He and his two wives lie there in state on their massive canopied tomb, and there are stone doves – what else? – perched above them.

It is divided from the nave by an elegant stone balustrade with three stone steps up to it, appropriate for a superior garden terrace but a little odd in these surroundings. Nowadays I doubt it would get further than the drawing-board, but in the seventeenth century, if you were Lord of the Manor and your father was a bishop, nobody argued. Happily, the rails and balusters around the altar table are in hand-carved wood, dating back to the time when Archbishop Laud decreed that rails be installed in sanctuaries to stop dogs profaning the altar.

At one time there was a crypt under the north aisle, and local legend has it that a tunnel connected it with the manor house, a couple of hundred yards away. Nobody seems to know where it is – which is a pity, because legend also has it that the bishop hid the cathedral treasure in it during the Civil War, and there might still be some left. The manor house has been replaced by a farm-house, and the terraced garden which linked it with the church is now grazed by sheep. What does survive, however, is a curious lump of stone, carved into strange shapes, midway between farmhouse and church. It is recorded as being a sundial from the time of Charles I, but the gnomons have long since gone, and nobody quite knows how it works. Indeed it is difficult to recognize as a sundial at all.

My own theory is that this function was only secondary, and it was carved in this curious fashion to distract Cromwell's treasure-hunters and give them something else to think about. It was primarily an air vent for that tunnel.

RIGHT Sir William Dove and his wives lie in state in their canopied tomb, with a flight of doves instead of angels.

18 miles E of Chelmsford off B1021

Britain's oldest cathedral survived 1300 years – then the RAF nearly used it as a target

ST PETER'S MAY LOOK LIKE AN OLD barn – certainly the RAF thought so, and it was actually used for that purpose for years – but in fact it can claim to be the oldest cathedral in the country, built by Bishop Cedd in AD 654. And in spite of its isolated position on the edge of the marshes, well away from the village and only accessible across the fields, its services are well attended and it attracts many hundreds of visitors each year.

It was even more remote when St Cedd sailed down the coast from Lindisfarne, at the invitation of King Sigbert of the East Saxons, to bring Christianity to the pagans of Essex. He found the ruins of a Roman fort and used the stones to build a little monastery on the old Roman wall. For the next five or six years he used it as his base while he set up churches from Mersea to Tilbury, and a little community in wooden huts grew up around the main building which served as a social centre and a hospital as well as a place of worship. Then he was recalled to the North to set up another monastery at Lastingham, but St Peter's continued to function for another two centuries, until the Essex coast came under constant attack from Viking raiders, and it was allowed to fall into ruin.

For a time it was used as a smugglers' hideaway, until the local farmer knocked entrances in the walls for his farm carts and used it as a barn. The outline of those entrances can still be seen, but it has now been restored for use as a chapel. The mod-

ern altar has three stones set in it from the other three monasteries connected with St Cedd – the parent monastery at Iona, Lindisfarne where he was educated and ordained, and Lastingham where he is buried.

Having survived for thirteen centuries, St Peter's nearly met an untimely end during the last war – not from enemy bombers, but our own. The commander of the local RAF station happened to meet the rector one morning, and they discussed the sta-

tion's training programme. 'This morning,' said the CO, 'we are having a little target practice. We are going to knock out that old barn in the field over there …'

The rector explained, with some urgency, that they would then be destroying the oldest cathedral in the country. The CO cancelled the exercise, and St Peter's was saved, thanks to that chance encounter. But was it, one wonders, entirely by chance? Could it have happened because of something Cedd said – in the right quarter?

RIGHT St Peter's had a last-minute reprieve; was it something Cedd said?

2 miles SW of Brentwood on the B186

'No, I won't give a donation: I'll just give you a church' – and what a church it was

AT FIRST SIGHT, AS YOU PASS THROUGH the traditional lychgate and walk through the traditional churchyard, there seems nothing untraditional about St Mary's itself. It has the familiar rough-cast walls, the familiar porch, the familiar belfry and shingled spire. Only the metal Dove of Peace, perched on the spire, gives a hint of what lies inside.

At the turn of this century the original St Mary's was crumbling away, and a subscription list was opened to build a new one. An approach was made to Evelyn Heseltine, a stockbroker who had created 'a large manorial estate, somewhat feudal in concept'. The story goes that he said he would not subscribe – but if they liked, he would give them a new church. At the Easter Vestry in 1901 the news was received with acclama-tion; they did not know, of course, what sort of church they would be getting …

It is primarily the work of the sculptor and interior designer Sir William Reynolds-Stephens. In St Mary's he created the ultimate in art nouveau, using materials which would have staggered earlier church-builders, even if they had ever heard of them. Here is just a flavour.

The font is white marble on a black marble dais, with bronze angels and a metal cover inlaid with mussel pearl. The pendant lights, or 'electroliers', are galvanized iron with enamel panels. The pulpit is made of beaten sheets of various metals riveted together (the rivets are part of the decorations), with bronze trees growing up it from a black marble podium. The rood screen has brass rose-trees rooted in dark green marble with flowers of mother-of-pearl and fruits made of enamel. Even the roof has ribs finished in aluminium leaf. The whole effect is quite astonishing.

One lonely figure to survive from the original church is Gyles Fleming, one of the much earlier squires of Great Warley. His bust stares wide-eyed in utter disbelief. 'For a time,' says the guidebook, 'Guy was deposited in the right-hand corner of the church porch, but since he presented a somewhat startling countenance to the hurrying latecomer, it was decided to put him back under cover.' He is now in the vestry, trying not to think about his nouveau surroundings.

BELOW Mother-of-pearl flowers and enamel fruits on the brass rood screens.

7 miles N of Brentwood off the A128

The experts may argue about dates, but it is still the oldest wooden church in the world

ST ANDREW'S PROUDLY CLAIMS TO BE the oldest wooden church in the world – but it discovered a few years ago that it may not be quite as old as it thought. Until then its wooden walls were dated about AD845, but fresh tests showed they were probably rebuilt a couple of hundred years later, just before the Conquest. Even so, it still claims the record.

It was probably allowed to survive by the Normans – who preferred stone churches to wooden ones – because it was a sacred shrine to St Edmund, the Saxon king who was shot to death with arrows and beheaded by the Danes for refusing to renounce his faith. He died in Suffolk, but his body was taken to London for safe keeping. In 1013 it was brought back, and the cortège rested at St Andrew's on their way to bury St Edmund – at Bury St Edmunds. His martyrdom is featured in one of the windows, and a carved beam over the nave illustrates the legend of a wolf guarding his severed head until his followers retrieved it.

A curious niche in one of the upright staves in the south wall was at one time

BELOW The matyrdom of St Edmund. His funeral cortege rested here on its way to Bury St Edmunds.

thought to be a leper's squint, but it is only about three feet above the ground, and all you can see through it is the door in the opposite wall, instead of the priest at the altar. The more likely theory is that it was a stoup for holy water by a Saxon door, now blocked up.

St Andrew's has an unusual link with the Tolpuddle Martyrs, the Dorset farm-workers who were sent to Australia for trying to form a trade union. When they were allowed to return, the Dorset farmers would not have them, and they were granted tenancies in and around Greensted. One of them, James Brine, married the daughter of a fellow martyr, Elizabeth Standfield, at St Andrew's. It is recorded in the church register for 1839 – and also on one of the hassocks. Unfortunately the rector shared the views of the Dorset farm-ers and prevented their tenancies being renewed, so they sailed away again – this time on a voluntary basis – and settled in Canada.

They fared rather better than a local Greensted farm-worker, whose cross in the churchyard, like the church itself, is wooden instead of stone. He used to scythe the grass there, but one day he drank too much beforehand, the scythe cut his legs instead of the grass, and he bled to death. The moral, so they say in Greensted with rather grisly humour, is: 'Don't ask a man to drink and scythe …'

RIGHT The Saxon log walls are now surmounted by later dormer windows, but St Andrew's still claims to be our oldest wooden church

5 miles N of Saffron Walden on the B1052

They once nailed a visitor's skin on the door: now the biggest hazard is the maze

IF HADSTOCK WAS THE ICANHO WHERE St Botolph built his monastery – as everyone in Hadstock believes – then his church has had a sort of love-hate relationship with the Danes for over a thousand years. Icanho and the monastery were burnt down by the Great Army of the Danes in 870. Then along came the Danish King Canute in 1016, defeated the Saxon Edmund Ironside, and built a minster in memory of those slain in the battle. It is said to have been on the site of the monastery and became the present St Botolph's. Certainly the main door dates from that period, confirmed in the *Guinness Book of Records* as the oldest door in use in Britain.

Tradition also has it that a Dane was flayed alive for sacrilege at about this time, and his skin was nailed on the door – and in this case there is evidence to prove it. When the door was repaired, a piece of human skin was found under one of the hinges. It is now in Saffron Walden Museum.

The Danish connection continued over the centuries – rather more pleasantly. St Botolph was superseded in Britain by St Christopher as the patron saint of travellers, but he is still the patron saint of Danish fishermen. Hadstock established a link in 1790 with St Budolphi Cathedral at Aalborg, and in 1995 the Danish Embassy presented

RIGHT The gravestone of Michel Ayrton, master mazebuilder. His maze is based on the original Labyrinth.

the church with the Danish flag which hangs in the north transept, alongside that of St George.

The Danes' reputation for rape and pillage was probably exaggerated, but the idea may have caught on at St Botolph's – the pillage, anyway. The oak lectern is thought to have been plundered from a monastery after the Dissolution, and in 1790, when the chancel fell into ruins, the parishioners carted away the stones for their own use, provoking an appalled reaction from the bishop. 'Since I have been upon the Episcopal Bench I have known of no instance of a chancel being entirely taken away ...' The rector gamely accepted responsibility and built a modest new one at his own expense.

St Botolph's most unusual feature in modern times, however, is linked more with the Greeks than the Danes. Michael Ayrton was a master maze-builder, and his headstone in the churchyard has a bronze plaque of the maze he built in America, based on the original Labyrinth occupied by the Minotaur. Visitors constantly run their fingers round it to see if they can trace the route to the centre. Having tried it, I think it could take them a very long time.

RIGHT Greensted may claim the oldest wooden walls, but St Botolph's claims the oldest door, and the Guinness Book of Records *backs it up. It was once decorated with the skin of a sacriligious Dane.*

7 miles NE of Colchester on the A137

Ghostly monks in procession on All Saints' Day: I never saw them, but I know a woman who did ...

ST MARY'S IS WELL AWAY FROM THE village, but in this case it cannot be blamed on the Black Death. It was an estate church, built in 1340 by Sir Benet de Cokefield of Lawford Hall, which is linked to St Mary's by an avenue of lime trees. The villagers, on the other hand, have had a fair old walk to church ever since. But it has also meant that the church was well endowed by Sir Benet's successors, right down to the present day. Only four families have been involved in all that time – the Waldegraves, the Dents, the Greens and the Nicholses – and their memorials are much in evidence.

St Mary's architecture covers the same period. Three centuries separate Sir Benet's stone chancel from the tower, which is faced in red brick, and another three separate the tower from the hall which was added in 1991. The hall is built to look like the chan-cel, and the block linking it to the church is rendered to match the north aisle; it all adds up to an interesting mixture of styles and materials.

Since the 1970s several new housing estates have increased Lawford's population considerably – hence the need for a hall – but none of them is anywhere near the church. It is still on a lonely site, and inevitably strange stories are told about it. Edna Sims, for instance, used to walk past it on her way home, when she was a young girl during the war. One night she saw flickering lights in the church, and took a peep through the door. She told me she saw a procession of cowled monks walking down the aisle, carrying candles, swinging incense, and chanting.

'It all looked so real. I told the rector next day and he said, You must have gone back in time, my dear; yesterday was All Saints' Day.'

The present rector, the Revd Peter Ball, does not discount the story. 'Edna is very sensitive, and I am sure she is wholly genuine in what she claims to have seen. My predecessor saw two ghost-like figures in the churchyard – and I have no reason to doubt his word. But I haven't seen a thing.'

Other strange stories, however, are less well authenticated; they have no doubt got stranger over the years. I noticed that one of the chancel's eight windows is decorated differently from the others: it depicts little men frolicking, and each one holds a leg of the man above him. Even in the fourteenth century, it seems, it was not unknown for the locals to pull each other's legs ...

BELOW A mixture of styles in the windows.

1 miles SW of Colchester off the A12

Like other Victorian rectors he was allowed a free hand – and his hand held a paintbrush

LITTLE BRAXTED IS SO LITTLE THAT IT doesn't even appear on some maps, and St Nicholas's was a very little church – and one of the most unremarkable – until the Revd Ernest Geldart became rector in the 1880s. He was an architect as well as a cleric, and considerably enlarged the church. He was also a painter, and perhaps one reason that he enlarged it was to create a bigger canvas for his painting. In three years he covered every wall, every pillar, every archway, until this previously traditional little English country church had been given a brightly decorated Byzantine interior, literally wall-to-wall.

Some of it looks very like the ostentatiously-patterned wallpaper favoured by the Victorians – but in their living-rooms, not their churches. There are saints and angels too, more patterns on the ceiling, and inscriptions in Gothic lettering on every available beam or arch, some of them familiar texts, others almost incomprehen-sible. But every pattern, every figure, every inscription has some special significance: the trick is to work out what it is.

At the time, nobody seemed to object. Victorian parsons with money to spare had a free hand – even when the hand held a paintbrush. But in more recent times, when the paintings needed restoring and

BELOW AND RIGHT The traditional English exterior of St Nicholas's and the Revd Ernest Geldart's brightly decorated interior.

money was required to do it, there was considerable disquiet among the parishioners. Peggy Church, an aptly-named church councillor, recalled that time.

'Once they saw it finished, most of the objectors changed their minds,' she told me, 'but there were still some who thought it was a great waste of money; they would have preferred the walls to be white-washed. But it would have been sacrilege to get rid of all this. It may be a distraction when people come the first time and try to take it all in, and perhaps that takes away from their spiritual thoughts, but on the other hand the intention of it is to teach, and you have to take quite a long time to find out all the hidden meanings. You look

at them, and it is part of your worship in a way …'

There is one other curious feature of St Nicholas's which is not quite as striking as the paintings. When it was built and dedicated to St Nicholas, they wanted the sunlight to shine directly through the east window on the day of his patronal festival, December 6th. Unfortunately at that time of year the sunrise is not due east of Little Braxted, and the church was built slightly askew. So the east window is not actually east but east-ish.

BELOW AND RIGHT More Examples of the Revd Ernest Geldart's artistry. He covered the walls, the pillars, the archway, the ceiling …

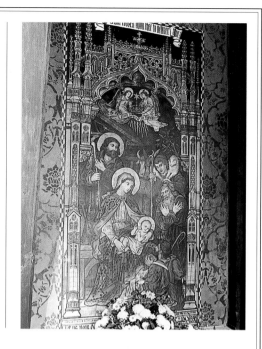

10 miles S of Colchester off the B1026

Racing yachts in the window, an American lady bell-captain – and the swearing font

TOLLESBURY HAS ALWAYS BEEN A sailing community, and St Mary's reflects this maritime connection, from the sailing ship weathervane on the tower to the 'Seafarers' Window' in the nave. Tollesbury men were in the crews of nearly all the sixteen British contenders for the America's Cup, including two skippers, and four of their yachts and schooners are portrayed in the window. On the other side are examples of the less glamorous craft that sailed in local coastal waters – a ketch-rigged barge, an oyster smack, an all-purpose 'billy boy' and a 'stackie', built to carry hay and straw to London. The window was given by an American, Mr F. E. Hasler of New York, in 1963.

These days St Mary's has another transatlantic connection. The bell-captain is an American, Nan Wilson, who has assembled an almost all-women team to ring the unique church bells – the lightest peal of ten bells in the country. The first six were hung in 1633, two more were added in 1967 when a new metal frame was installed, and the final two were hung in 1990. One of them bears the name of Nan Wilson, one of the few Americans to have a memorial in her own lifetime in the belfry of an English country church.

And an ancient country church at that. It dates back to the eleventh

RIGHT The 'Swearing Font', donated as a penance by an eighteenth-century drunk who swore in church.

century, and its builders incorporated two splays of brickwork, still visible, using bricks made by the Romans. Christianity was brought to this part of England in the seventh century by Bishop Cedd, who built the chapel of St Peter at Bradwell, just across the estuary, and a small window in St Mary's depicts him holding the chapel in his hand. The chapel itself is still in use, the oldest 'cathedral' in England.

St Mary's cannot compete with that distinction, but it does have its Swearing Font. It's not the font that swears, of course, but the man who paid for it. The inscription reads: 'Good people, all I pray take care, that in ye church you doe not sware. As this man did.' John Norman was an eighteenth-century drunk who 'cursed and talked aloud in the time of Divine Service', and to avoid being prosecuted he donated £5 for a new font. The first baby was baptized in it in 1718.

Some of these tales about country churches can be a little difficult to accept, but the story of the Swearing Font is absolutely true. I swear.

LEFT The 'Seafarers' Window'. It has some of the British contenders in the America's Cup, manned by Tollesbury men, and less glamorous craft which used to sail in local waters.

6 miles NE of Baldock off the A505

Graffiti can be acceptable – if they are in Latin and six hundred years old

SCRIBBLING ON WALLS IS GENERALLY frowned upon in churches, but in St Mary's the graffiti are probably its most famous feature. It makes all the difference when the scribbling was done six centuries ago, by Latin scholars with sharp instruments and in some cases an even sharper wit. These graffiti, in fact, are distinctly up-market.

The most significant are in the choir vestry in the tower. One inscription translates: 'Miserable, wild, distracted, the dregs of the people alone survive to witness'; it refers to the bubonic plague which swept through the country and terrified the population during the fourteenth century. A second refers to another national disaster: 'And in the end a tempest full mighty; this year 1361 St Maur thunders in the world' – a graphic description of a devastating storm on St Maurice's Day, 15 January.

But the graffito which interests archaeologists most is not a message but a meticulous drawing of the original St Paul's Cathedral, before its spire fell down in 1561.

Other graffiti in the church are less important, but rather more fun. On one pillar a master mason expresses his disgust at his men's work: 'The corners are not pointed correctly – I spit.' The workmen might not know Latin, but they would recognize the word 'sputo'. And on another pillar there is a pungent punning comment on an obviously irritating lady:

'Barbara filia Barbara est' – in effect, 'Barbara by name, barbarian by nature.'

In addition to all this informative and sometimes entertaining medieval vandalism, St Mary's has much more to offer, from the tallest tower in Hertfordshire – 177 feet high with the little spirelet on top – to the impressive modern cross above the altar, made by a president of the Royal Society of British Sculptors. The embroidered altar reredos is, surprisingly, the work

of a former verger, Mr Percy Sheldrick.

Compared with these – and the graffiti – the church clock may seem fairly average, but it too has a tale to tell. When it was installed in 1896, an adjoining farmer objected to having a face on his side of the tower in case his men wasted their time clock-watching. That is why there are only three faces – and why residents on the fourth side may have been late for work ever since …

RIGHT The original St Paul's Cathedral before its spire fell down in 1561 – one of the church's treasured graffiti.

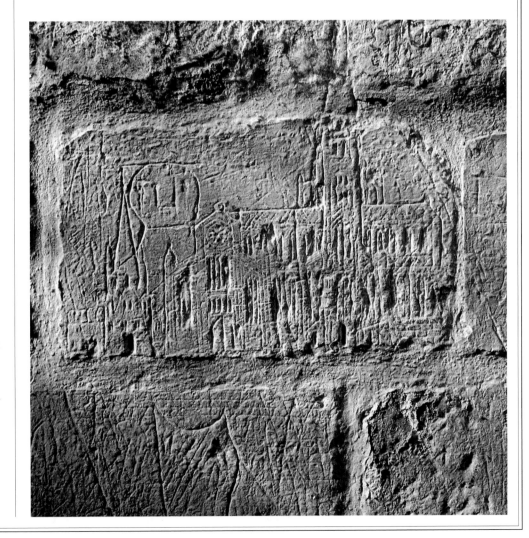

3 miles NW of Welwyn Garden City off the B656

He wrecked one church and built another, facing the wrong way – just to improve his view

SIR LIONEL LYTE WAS ONE OF THOSE squires in the 1770s who would knock down a whole village if it spoilt his view. In his case it was not the village but the thirteenth-century church, and he had half-demolished it before the bishop found out and stopped him. By then he had knocked down enough to see the site of his new church, and he went about building it with the same high-handed disregard for the conventions. It looks more like a Greek temple than a traditional country church, with a massive pillared portico and colonnades on each side, leading to little open pavilions. And to make sure he saw the portico and not the other end of the church, which was left virtually undecorated, he had it built the wrong way round, which means the altar is at the west end instead of the east.

The architect was Nicholas Revett, who built Sir Francis Dashwood's elaborate church at West Wycombe, but at Ayot he kept the pillars outside the church and left the walls of the nave uncluttered. There is a lofty domed sanctuary – at the wrong end, of course – and at the other, over the

BELOW The sanctuary is at the west end instead of the east, so the squire could enjoy a better view.

entrance, there is a balcony where Sir Lionel and his family were seated during services. From this vantage point he could look down at the congregation, count heads, see who was missing, and make a note to find out why.

To do him justice, he spared no expense – though present-day parishioners may feel he could have spent it better on some kind of heating. The roof is of copper sheeting and the elegant organ with its mahogany frame is considered a fine example of the period. The pavilions at the far ends of the colonnades were built, it seems, with a specific purpose in mind. One contains Sir Lionel's remains, the other contains his wife's. Apparently it was not the happiest of marriages, and Sir Lionel took the view that, since the Church had been responsible for uniting them in life, it could make amends by separating them in death.

Ayot St Lawrence's other famous figure, George Bernard Shaw, was hardly a great church-goer, but apparently it was a tombstone in the churchyard which prompted him to move to the village. It commemorated a lady who had died aged seventy, and the epitaph read simply: 'Her time was short'. Bernard Shaw decided that if the age of seventy was considered a short life in Ayot, this was the place for him.

He was right, of course. He lived there for forty-four years, and he was over ninety when he died. But judging by other tombstones, it hasn't always worked – so don't all rush...

RIGHT Sir Lionel's final resting place – as far from his wife as possible.

12 miles E of Stevenage, off the B1030

Did the double-sided coat of arms lead a double life?

THE CHURCHES AT BRENT PELHAM and Furneux Pelham were first linked in the twelfth century by the Bishop of London, who put them under the jurisdiction of the Treasurer of St Paul's. It was only in 1877 that St Paul's agreed to hand over their control to the diocese of St Albans. They are in separate benefices now, but they still share an interest – or so it is said at Brent Pelham – in the unusual double-sided Royal coat of arms in Furneux church. The lion and unicorn each have two heads, facing each way, so the coat of arms looks exactly the same on both sides.

At Furneux they say it was installed after the Restoration by the Royalist rector, who had patrolled the churchyard during the Civil War to repel any marauding Roundheads. There are mutterings at Brent Pelham, however, that it was originally in their church, and was mysteriously transferred. They could possibly both be right.

Fortunately each St Mary's has its own treasures which are not disputed. Furneux, for instance, has a splendid old parish chest in the priest's room over the porch, now used for Sunday School. The only mystery is how it got in there, because experts say it is older than the porch, yet it is too bulky to have come through the doorway or the windows. Could this be the only church, one wonders, to be built around a parish chest?

Brent Pelham can counter this with the equally unlikely story of Piers Shonks, a thirteenth-century local hero who slew an evil dragon, and was buried in the wall of the church so his soul could not be taken by the Devil. The story seems to be confirmed by the carved dragon on his tomb, with the

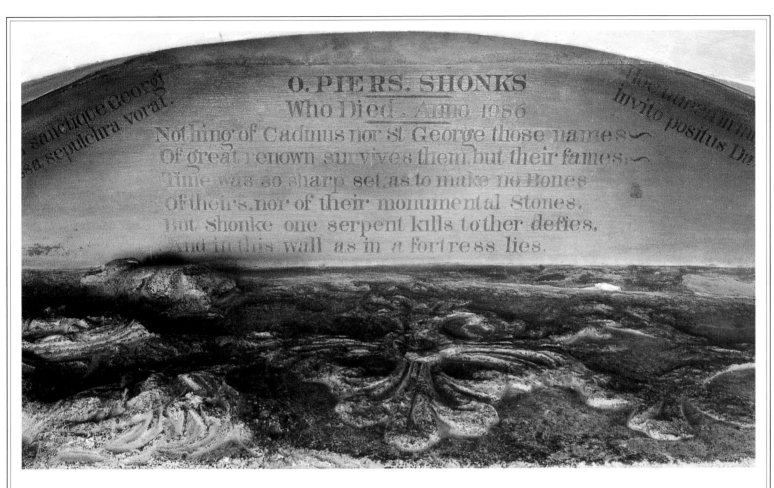

O. PIERS. SHONKS
Who Died . Anno 1086
Nothing of Cadmus nor St George those names
Of great renown survives them but their fames;
Time was so sharp set as to make no Bones
Of their's nor of their monumental Stones,
But shonke one serpent kills tother defies,
And in this wall as in a fortress lies.

ABOVE AND RIGHT The tomb of Piers Shanks the Dragon-killer at Brent Pelham, and the ancient parish chest at Furneux Pelham.
LEFT The double-sided coat of arms at Furneux Pelham – but was it always there?

hilt of a sword emerging from its mouth, and a seventeenth-century parson helped to perpetuate the tale by inscribing a verse which ends: 'Shonks one serpent kills, t'other defies'. But sceptics have suggested that it is just a legend symbolizing good overcoming evil, and the sword-hilt in the dragon's mouth is actually a cross.

Personally I would vote for the dragon-slaying hero – and for the church being built round the parish chest. But perhaps I should take the advice inscribed on the church tower at Furneux Pelham – though it was probably not meant to be as curt as it sounds: 'Mind Your Own Business' …

9 miles SE of Canterbury off the A2

Carvings, carvings everywhere – but where did they put the bell?

ALL THE EXPERTS AGREE ON THE magnificence of the carvings at St Nicholas's Church – 'unique', 'beautifully worked', 'among the finest in Kent/England/Europe' – and even the humblest layman must be impressed by their quality, and variety, and sheer profusion. What is not so clear is why all this time and talent – and presumably hard cash – was expended on such an obscure little country church.

Barfrestone is not associated with great wealth. It has always been a quiet little village, notable only for its bracing climate – the name means 'cold bleak town' – and resulting from it, perhaps, the longevity of its inhabitants. St Nicholas's has seen some notable gatherings of geriatrics, not least the funeral of a rector who died in 1700 at the age of 96. The officiating priests, the sexton and the parish clerk were all in their eighties, and several of the mourners were centenarians.

But that can hardly be linked with the carvings. Remarkable though they are, nobody has yet credited them with the power to prolong life. So why are they there? Some say the masons belonged to the same guild as those who built Canterbury Cathedral, less than ten miles away, and my own theory is that the church was used by apprentice masons to perfect their skills. They could get practical experience of all kinds of subjects, from mythical beasts to saints and martyrs, and if they got bored they could invent their own cameos, like the monkey riding on a goat and carrying a dead hare. The experts have read symbolic meanings into most of the carvings at St Nicholas's, but I think that one has them beaten. It looks as though the master mason said to his pupils: 'If it moves, carve it – and if there's a space, fill it.' And they did.

So by all means marvel at this wealth of medieval masonry, as indeed I have marvelled myself. But I confess I was more taken with a touch of improvisation by some anonymous handyman which the experts are inclined to ignore. It seems the masons spent so much time and energy on their carvings, they omitted to provide St Nicholas's with a tower or even a bell-cote. But it does have a bell. It hangs in a yew tree in the churchyard, and it is rung with a rope which passes through the wall of the church. Not very artistic or symbolic – but it works.

ABOVE AND BELOW St Nicholas's is justly proud of its carvings, but its 'belfry' is quite remarkable too.

3 miles N of Westerham on the A233

'The moving church' – and the dust-covered lorry-driver in the dog-collar who moved it

THE BRICK AND BATH STONE CHURCH of St Mark's, with its separate, fortress-like campanile, is not your average country church – for a very good reason. It started off as a town church, in south-east London. Thanks to the inspiration of one man, the Revd Vivian Symons, army officer turned parish priest, the redundant church of All Saints', North Peckham, was almost miraculously transformed into St Mark's, Biggin Hill.

The story of 'The Moving Church' is the stuff that legends are made of. Until the arrival of Vivian Symons as Perpetual Curate in 1951 (Biggin Hill did not rate a vicar then), there was just a 'temporary' corrugated-iron church built in 1904 when Biggin Hill had a population of two hundred. By the 1950s, largely due to the establishment of Biggin Hill RAF station, it had risen to about four thousand, and the well-worn little church only seated seventy.

Symons, 'a small dark Cornishman of bounding vitality and unquenchable faith', decided to do something about it. He obtained permission to take over All Saints', cadged a lorry, and drove it in and out of London with a team of volunteers. They dismantled and loaded 125,000 bricks, 200 tons of stonework, all the roof timbers and 2 ½ miles of roof boarding, and drove it out to Biggin Hill. There the ladies of the parish divided their time between cleaning and stacking the bricks, and embroidering pew covers and hassocks.

The task of reassembling the new church

was too much for amateurs, but a local builder offered to erect it on a non-profit basis. Vivian Symons himself operated a borrowed jib crane to lift the final roof trusses into position. The new church was consecrated on St Mark's Day, 1959.

He died in 1976, but there are many reminders of him in the church, not least the fifty-odd windows on which he engraved biblical scenes – with a dentist's drill! A memorial tablet pays tribute to this 'soldier, priest and craftsman' in the simplest of terms: 'Through his faith and work this church was built.' But in a sense it is superfluous. As they say of Christopher Wren in St Paul's: 'His memorial is all around us.'

Perhaps the most memorable tribute came from a Londoner in a Camberwell café who saw a dust-covered lorry-driver in a clerical collar climb down from his cab and come in for a cup of tea. He commented loudly: 'Cor, now I've seen everything!' In Biggin Hill they reckon they have seen everything too …

RIGHT One of the windows engraved by Vivian Symons with a dentist's drill.

6 miles NE of Rye on the A259

The 'candle-snuffer' with tales to tell
– and so has the pulpit

SOME OF THE STORIES ATTACHED to St Augustine's 'candle–snuffer' belfry are even stranger than the belfry itself. It is said, for instance, that originally it was on the church, but after it had blown off a couple of times they got fed up with putting it back again. Then there is a variation on the story sometimes linked with a crooked spire; it was so amazed to see a confirmed old bachelor marrying an elderly spinster that it jumped down (instead of twisting) to get a closer look. There is also a tradition that Cardinal Wolsey moved it there from Lydd – but no one seems to know why.

The real story is more mundane, but still unique. The belfry started off in the twelfth century as just a framework for one big bell, to be used at times of flood or invasion. Then more bells were added three centuries later, with a conical weatherboard roof. The roof has been shingled since the 1930s, but its eleven thousand cedar shingles are still supported by some of the original beams.

Many people admire the belfry, then move on, but St Augustine's has other remarkable features – not least, the white shutter-gates in the porch, more often found in stables than churches. Inside, the arcades dividing the nave from the aisles lean at an alarming angle – but they have done for centuries, due to subsidence in the marshy soil. There is still a slight movement – half an inch in the last eighty years – but nobody seems too perturbed.

Foremost among the church's rare antiquities is the twelfth-century decorated lead font, possibly stolen from a French church by marauding English sailors. And there is a recently-uncovered wall-painting depicting the assassination of Thomas à Becket. But other churches have rare fonts and paintings: rarer still, perhaps, is one of the oldest surviving sets of measures for the corn, wine and cloth, which were paid to the rector as tithes.

Finally, the two-decker pulpit has a tale to match those of the candle-snuffer belfry. A rector started publishing the banns of marriage while still looking for the banns book. 'I publish the banns of marriage between…' and as he paused, still searching, a loud prompt came from the clerk below: '… between the cushion and the desk.'

BELOW the unusual white shutter-gates in the porch
RIGHT the 'candle-snuffer' belfry.

6 miles W of Ramsgate on the B2048

The story behind Ermenburga's window, of Uncle Egbert and the long-distance deer

THE FOUNDING OF ST MARY'S IS A delightful story involving a wicked uncle who repented, his wicked thane who didn't, a saintly but shrewd princess – and one of the few sponsored runs in history by a pet deer. The princess and the deer are in a stained-glass window in St Mary's, but strangely the church guide omits to mention the story behind them. So here it is …

In the seventh century the two brothers of Princess Ermenburga were murdered by Thurnor, the thane of her uncle, King Egbert, presumably on his master's instructions. But Egbert felt sorry for Ermenburga and offered her 'wegild', which these days would be called compensatory damages. She said she intended building a nunnery, and asked for as much land as her pet hind could encompass without a stop. Egbert agreed, and the hind set off. One suspects it had been in training for this event, because it kept going so long that Thurnor the thane decided – or was ordered? – to stop it earning any more land for Ermenburga. So he tried to cut it off, but his horse fell into a pit and he was drowned; some say the pit still exists nearby. The hind encompassed a thousand acres before eventually stopping for breath.

Egbert stood by his deal, Ermenburga got her land and built her nunnery under her religious name of Domneva. It included a church dedicated to St Mary. The window in the present St Mary's shows her with her

RIGHT Princess Ermenburgha's long-distance deer. Its stamina won her a thousand acres for her monastery.

daughter Mildred, the second abbess, who is holding a model of the nunnery. The guidebook says who they are, but it doesn't mention the deer in the panel below – the clue to the whole story.

There is no lack of other information about the church and its six architectural styles, going back to the Norman tower with its Saxon turret, which incorporates Roman tiles from an even earlier building era. For the non-expert, though, the most fascinating feature – apart from that window

– is the assortment of fifteenth-century misericords in the choir stalls, ranging from the head of Christ flanked by two wild-eyed monks to a woman wearing a scold's bridle.

There is also a roughly-scratched inscription on a nearby pillar which says: 'Let him learn who does not know, that Mr Trotman lies below.' Here too the guidebook does not give the story behind it – and this time I cannot help. Unless perhaps 'Mr Trotman' was Princess Ermenburga's pet name for her long-trotting deer?

2 miles E of Tonbridge on the B2017

'Obscure and unfrequented'
– but that was before Marc Chagall

IN 1798 A TRAVEL WRITER DESCRIBED All Saints' as 'obscure and unfrequented', and it stayed that way until about thirty years ago. But these days it is one of the few 'obscure and unfrequented' village churches which find it appropriate to print on the cover of its guide, not just 'Welcome!' but also 'Bienvenue … Bien venido … Wilkommen … Benvenuto …'

All Saints' does indeed attract visitors from all over Europe. They do not come to see its rather unendearing red-brick tower with the incongruous little spirelet on top, nor its fairly sparse collection of memorials, nor even its eighteenth-century marbled ceiling. What they all want to see are the windows, particularly the great East window, which were installed between 1967 and 1985 and designed by the world-famous Marc Chagall.

It all started tragically, with a sailing accident off Rye in 1963. Sarah Venetia, the young daughter of Sir Henry and Lady d'Avigdor-Goldsmid, who lived in the village, was drowned. Sir Henry, distinguished soldier, MP and racehorse-owner, commissioned Marc Chagall to design a memorial East window. It was made in Rheims and dedicated at All Saints' in 1967.

But this was only part of the memorial to Sarah Venetia. Her family and friends paid for the restoration of the church, including its marble ceiling, and Sir Henry commissioned more windows. Seven were installed in 1974, and Chagall, by this time entering his nineties, designed four more for the chancel. This last group was installed in 1985, the year of Chagall's death, so in a way they were a memorial to him too. 'The result', says the guide with justifiable pride, 'is an unparalleled collection of the works of Chagall in England.'

As to their precise meaning, that is for each visitor to decide. Perhaps the easiest to interpret is the original one, the East window, which portrays Christ on the Cross above a turbulent sea, with grieving figures and a messenger climbing the ladder to the Cross. The chestnut horse prancing above the waves may need more explaining. One might assume it is connected with the family's love of horses; the guide just says is symbolizes happiness – and leaves it at that.

RIGHT Marc Chagall's memorial window to a drowned girl, depicting Christ on the Cross above a troubled sea.

6 miles SW of Maidstone on the B2010

A weather-vane that perched on an onion
– and a bomb-blast that grew into a tree

ONE OF THE ODDEST RELICS IN ANY church must be the misshaped 'onion', which now sits, rather disconsolately, on a table by the font in St Peter's and St Paul's. It could be a mystery object in a 'Bygones' series; it is in fact known as the Elizabethan Onion, which used to stand proudly on the point of the minaret roof of the tower, supporting the weathervane. In 1967 it was declared dangerous and replaced, but the weathervane itself, bearing the date 1734, still swings above the tower.

The church clock was installed at about the same time as the weathervane, but it had no onion – and no minute hand. That was added more than a century later, when presumably the clockwatching residents of Yalding needed more precise guidance.

Other church features have not survived so long, notably the stained-glass windows, most of which were shattered when a German 'doodle-bug' exploded nearby during the last war. However, the most interesting windows were installed long after the war was over – though they commemorate, in part, the earlier war of 1914–18.

At the turn of the century a new headmaster came to run the village school, bringing a four-year-old son. The boy went on to Cleaves Grammar School, founded in 1665 by William Cleave, who gave his lands and houses in Yalding towards a free school for the parish; he is commemorated on the benefactors' board in the vestry. The school was closed in 1921, but its most famous pupil, after serving in the First World War, lived on to become known as 'The Poet of Peace and War'.

Edmund Blunden knew firsthand the grimness and desolation of the trenches, and did much to dispel the romance which some tried to attach to them. After he died in 1975 his great friend Laurence Whistler – whose elder brother Rex was killed in that war – engraved the Blunden memorial windows in St Peter's and St Paul's.

One depicts a trench, with a bomb exploding into bloom like a tree, and rusty barbed wire twisting into a living briar. In the other he simply sets out three verses from Blunden's 'Report on Experience'. One verse reads:

> *I have seen a green country*
> *   useful to the race*
> *Knocked silly with guns and mines,*
> *   its villages vanished,*
> *Even the last rat and last kestrel*
> *   banished –*
> *God bless us all,*
> *   this was peculiar grace …*

Few churches have a more telling memorial.

RIGHT Edmund Blunden's memorial window, designed by his great friend Laurence Whistler.

3 miles W of Norwich off the B1108

His shrine has gone, his well looks like Jack and Jill's – but his saintliness lives on

ST WALSTAN WAS A LOCAL BOY WHO not only made good, he did good – to such a degree that when he was buried here in 1016, the bishop, an assortment of priors and forty-odd monks were at the service. His shrine in the north transept became a place of pilgrimage for centuries, until it was destroyed in the Reformation and his relics burnt. Only the outline of the Shrine Chapel, as it was called, remains today, but the filled-in archway which led to it can still be seen in St Mary and St Walstan's, guarded by a little modern carving of Walstan, armed with his scythe.

Walstan left his prosperous home in Bawburgh when he was twelve to work as a farm labourer in Taverham, on the far side of a dense forest. He gave away all his possessions, even down to the shoes off his feet, and walked barefoot through stubble and thorns without injury or pain. All he retained were two oxen and a cart, which he was told in a vision would come in handy when he died: they were to carry him to his place of burial.

After his death the oxen duly set off with his body, negotiated the dense forest, and by a happy chance finished up back in Bawburgh. A holy well appeared where they stopped, which was so renowned for its healing powers that the locals, being shrewd Norfolkmen, bottled it and sold it in Norwich market. The well is still there, in a farmyard near the church, protected by a low brick parapet and a little gabled roof which make it look more like Jack and Jill's

BELOW St Walstan's Well; the locals sold its holy water in Norwich Market.

well than a saintly one.

During the heyday of the pilgrimages Norwich Cathedral Priory took over St Mary's and St Walstan's, with its considerable income, and this connection proved useful when the little church fell on hard times in later years. In Charles I's reign, when it had become too dilapidated and dangerous for the parishioners to use, the cathedral paid for its restoration, and when it happened again in the late 1800s, it once more came to the rescue. As well as helping with the cost, the Dean and Chapter presented the old nave pulpit from the cathedral, which remains in use at St Mary's and St Walstan's.

The Saxon round tower still survives, and so does a curious poor-box dating from Henry II, which looks like a medieval traffic bollard. More importantly, St Walstan's memory prospers. He is widely recognized as the patron saint of agriculture, and in 1989 he was made patron of the British Food and Farming Year. Maybe the cathedral will find he is a very good investment again …

6 miles W of Wells-next-the-Sea on the A149

Not just a pretty font: it could have served as an instruction manual for medieval farmers

EACH OF THE SIX SURVIVING BURNHAM churches has something special about it, whether it be the display of biblical scenes and figures on the tower at Burnham Westgate, or the collection of Nelson memorabilia at Burnham Thorpe, where his father was rector, but I would select two others. One has a treasure which is among the finest of its kind in the country, the other contains a remarkable variety of unusual features. For me, Burnham Deepdale and Burnham Norton take the Burnham double-wafer biscuit. The Deepdale wafer first …

St Mary's has some surprises as soon as you enter the porch. The windows on each side feature faces representing the sun and the moon, as if you are entering some pagan temple. One window adds a bizarre note with the apparently unconnected enquiry, 'Death, where is they sting?' But these are actually fragments of ancient glass from other windows – something of a speciality in St Mary's – and the sun and moon probably originated from a Crucifixion scene. They would have appeared on each side of the Cross.

There are other bits-and-pieces windows inside. One in the north aisle, for example, has a merchant's mark at the top, to indicate the donor, but there is the word 'Geld' at the bottom, meaning a local guild gave it. The two pieces presumably came from different windows, and no one knows which of the other bits were donated by whom. They include assorted heads, a musical angel, the Holy Trinity, some roses, and Saint Ursula. Take your pick …

All these fragmented windows are reminders of the difficult times St Mary's has been through, but it has still retained, almost undamaged, its original early Norman font. Even this seems to have had its ups and downs – and its ins and outs. According to one work of reference, for forty years it was used as a garden cistern at Fincham rectory, twenty-five miles away. It does not explain how it got there, or why, or how it got back, but it has survived as one of the most noted fonts of its kind in the country. Around its sides are carved the Labours of the Month, showing the right time for digging, pruning, weeding, mowing, harvesting, threshing and grinding, with a pause in May for Rogationtide. In November it is time to kill a pig, in preparation for the feasting depicted in December.

It is in fact an early farming manual, showing how the seasons succeeded each other then, just as they do today – and just as the sun and moon succeed each other also. Perhaps those fragments in the porch windows are all part of the same story.

BELOW The Norman font illustrates the Labours of the Month; and the gardening tools involved – not a deckchair in sight.

5 miles W of Wells-next-the-Sea off the A149

An extra pulpit, an extra leg on the font – even an extra St Margaret

THE FIRST GREAT ADVANTAGE THAT St Margaret's has over the other Burnham churches is its position on a hillside away from the village, overlooking the salt marshes and the sea. That makes it a popular choice for weddings – and for funerals, as the extended churchyard testifies. But for me it is the sheer variety of its unusual and unlikely features.

For instance, it has twice the usual number of pulpits. One is pseudo-Jacobean, actually built in the last century from pieces of surplus wood found in the church. The other is a genuine and extremely rare pre-Reformation 'wineglass' pulpit, on a wooden stem so slender it is no longer safe for regular use. It is decorated with paintings of the four Latin Doctors and the two donors, John Goldale and his wife. Goldale was caught stealing oysters on the marshes and may well have given it as a penance.

There also seem to be two holy water stoups, one on each side of the door, but one is actually fitted with a chimney the width of the wall. It is a bread oven, once used for baking the Communion wafers. The church also has two St Margarets. The east window depicts the patron saint, St Margaret of Antioch, and beside her St Margaret of Scotland, whose daughter married Henry I. It is not explained why this eleventh-century Scottish queen is featured in a remote Norfolk church: perhaps the other St Margaret wanted female company, and the name seemed familiar.

RIGHT The rare 'wineglass' pulpit, possibly given as a penance for stealing oysters on the marshes.

The Norman font is not as elaborate as Deepdale's, but it has an odder feature – apparently a fifth leg in the middle. It is actually a well-disguised drain. The rood screen has an unusual decoration too, considering it dates from 1458: it bears the arms of Repton School and the 4th/7th Royal Dragoon Guards. The original paintings became defaced and unrecognizable, and in 1953 it was restored in memory of Lieut. R. D. Hancock, who died in the last war; hence the arms of his school and his army unit.

There are also reminders at St Margaret's of two gallant sailors who each became famous in their own fields. Lord Nelson's father and two brothers all feature on the list of rectors, and in the churchyard, under an imposing stone anchor, lies Captain Woodget, captain of the *Cutty Sark*. There are two Royal coats of arms, George IV's and Charles I's, the remains of a medieval wall-painting, and one of the most complete Saxon towers in Norfolk. And if you still want something else to look at after all that, then you have the marvellous view, a sweeping panorama of fields, salt marshes, sea and sky. No other Burnham can match it.

6 miles SW of Aylsham on the B1145

A pub sign is quite a rarity in church – but St Matthew seems too short-sighted to spot it

EXPERTS ARE DELIGHTED WITH St Agnes's great buttressed tower, and its medieval rood screen, and its hammerbeam roof, but it has less dramatic features which I find just as fascinating, and the stories behind the church are as remarkable as the church itself.

It was built at the end of the fourteenth century by the first Earl of Suffolk, Michael de la Pole – his family emblem, a 'wild man' or woodman, appears over the main door and on a piscina in one of the transepts. The freestone was brought from France and had to be carted from the nearest navigable river, nearly ten miles as the crow flies and a lot further as the cart is hauled. The cost should have been enormous, but apparently each parish through which the carts passed provided the labour to haul them. It seems remarkably philanthropic on their part, but could well have been fixed through the Old Landlords' Network; the earl had a word with his counterparts along the route, and they just told their serfs to get on with it …

The screen involved extra labour too – three artists instead of one, each with a slightly different style. My vote would go to the one who painted St Matthew – wearing glasses. I have not seen him portrayed like this elsewhere; perhaps in other paintings the short-sighted saint is wearing contact lenses.

While the screen needed three people to paint it, the ornate little poor-box needed three people to open it. Parish chests, which contained all manner of valuables, often had three different locks with different keys – one each for the rector and churchwardens – but it seems unusual for a poor-box to rate this precaution. The Church Council must have been an untrusting lot …

For me, though, the most delightful feature of St Agnes's is its Plough Gallery, plus an antiquated plough and the sign from the Plough Inn at Sygate, near the church, which was closed in 1950. It may be the only pub sign permanently on display in a country church. The gallery was installed by the medieval Plough Guild, which used to drag a plough round the village on Plough Monday, the twelfth day of Christmas, collecting donations for a final party at their headquarters (the Plough, naturally) before returning to work next morning. As the villagers always gave freely, to ensure a good harvest, it must have been quite a party; if the practice had continued, the Plough might never have had to close.

LEFT One of the few pub signs to hang inside a church; there is a real plough there too.

9 miles NW of Aylsham on the B1149

The rector found the church was a long way to cycle – so he moved it nearer

DURING THE BLACK DEATH IN 1349 the villagers of Edgefield evacuated their homes and moved to higher ground a mile away, leaving only the church behind. It became more and more neglected, and by the 1870s its chancel arch was sagging, the walls were crumbling, the pews were collapsing, and even the font had lost its pedestal. To the new rector it provided an opportunity not just to restore it but to rebuild it on a more convenient site.

Although Canon Walter Marcon was new to the living, he was hardly new to the village. He was born in the rectory in 1850, and after getting his degree and serving his curacy he came back and spent the rest of his life there, dying in the bed in which he was born. In 1877 he obtained a faculty from the bishop, persuaded the Marchioness of Lothian to give him a site in the village, organized a savings scheme in the parish to help raise the money, and started the work.

The main body of the old church was dismantled and re-erected in a faithful reconstruction, leaving just the tower and chancel behind. The medieval screens and old wall-monuments were reinstated, and even the font bowl was given a new pedestal. There was talk of restless spirits in the graveyard, disturbed by the removal of the church, but Canon Marcon pressed on. The new St Peter's and St Paul's was consecrated in 1884.

To mark the centenary in 1984 the Marcon Window was installed. It shows the new church, the old church tower, the two patronal saints, and Canon Marcon himself, in cassock and black hat, riding his bicycle to church – a rather shorter distance than when he first became rector. He left another reminder which is less public, a splendidly-bound diary which is held by the present rector, the Revd Keith Hawkes. He read me the inscription on the flyleaf:

'Edgefield rectory, July 1880. This book is the private property of me, Walter Herbert Marcon, and not of the parish or the church wardens. I wish my executors to give it after my death to the next incumbent, after he has been duly instituted. I beg him to make provision that it may never fall into other hands.'

Mr Hawkes told me: 'It is very private, it contains his deepest feelings – and I am afraid you cannot see it.' But one day, perhaps? What a story it may tell…

RIGHT Part of the Marcon window, showing the rector on his (shortened) bike ride to work.

12 miles SE of Cromer on the B1159

A churchyard for shipwrecked mariners, plus bizarre Mr Balls

VISITORS TO ST MARY'S MAY BE impressed most by its splendid fifteenth-century font, carved with a profusion of angels, assorted birds and animals, and brawny wodehouses, 'wild men of the woods'. But for mariners the church's key feature is its tower, 110 feet high and one of the best-known landmarks on that stretch of coast. Happisburgh's distinctive red-and-white lighthouse is another, but the two features have not always proved effective. The churchyard contains the graves of hundreds of sailors who have fallen foul of the notorious Haisbro Sands.

One mound marks the grave of 119 crew members of HMS *Invincible*, wrecked in 1801 on her way to join Nelson's fleet. Other casualties have included the crews of two Revenue cutters, on patrol for smugglers. HMS *Hunter* was destroyed by a storm in 1804 and the crew stood no chance; fifteen years later, when her successor HMS *Peggy* ran aground on a sandbank, it is said there were signals of distress and cries could be heard on shore, but nobody went to their aid. The villagers denied it, but there is no doubt that the Revenue men were none too popular along that coast.

Nor, as it turned out, was Jonathan Balls who was buried at St Mary's in 1846, but in a much more bizarre fashion. Mr Balls died of an unknown ailment, as had a number of his relatives and acquaintances in the village. At his own request he was buried with his Bible, a piece of plum cake, a poker

and a pair of tongs. However, this curious assortment was dug up again with his body when suspicions mounted that neither Mr Balls, nor his friends and acquaintances, had died of natural causes.

All of them were found to have traces of arsenic in their bodies, and it was decided that he had poisoned them all, then feared discovery and poisoned himself. Even so, when he was re-interred his wish was still observed and the same items were re-buried with him. If he indeed got his just desserts, the fireirons should have proved particularly useful …

RIGHT The fifteenth-century font with its club-wielding wodehouses, traditional wild men.

6 miles SE of Swaffham, off the B1077 (unmarked)

Derelict, forgotten, taken over by Satanists
– but its paintings survived

ST MARY'S IS ALL THAT REMAINS OF Houghton-on-the-Hill, which vanished many years ago – and the little Saxon church nearly vanished too. It was rediscovered during a Women's Institute outing, and the secretary happened to be the wife of Bob Davey, a local churchwarden and church enthusiast. She told him about the deserted, derelict church in the woods on Houghton Hill – with something very wrong about it. Mr Davey went to see.

'It was laid out as a Satanic temple,' he told me. 'Altar, fire, upside-down crosses, the sign of the goddess they worshipped … It was still a consecrated church, so of course that was a great attraction for them. Later they came back, smashed open a grave near the chancel with a pointed stake, and stole the skull and long-bones.'

The church roof was falling to bits and the tower was open to the sky. It was smothered in ivy and the churchyard was completely overgrown. Bob Davey virtually adopted St Mary's, rescued it from desecration, restored it as a building, and revived it as a church. He organized grants to repair the roof and make it weatherproof, while he personally cleared and replanted the churchyard. And in the course of all this, the great treasure of St Mary's was rediscovered, medieval wall-paintings which the experts say are among the oldest and best-preserved in the country.

They represent the Holy Trinity and the Crucifixion, and below is a row of saints

RIGHT Part of the re-discovered wall paintings, said to be the oldest and best-preserved in the country.

holding dead snakes, a sign they had conquered evil. There are two angels playing shawms, a kind of medieval oboe, and beneath all this is a crowd of people gazing upwards with hands together in prayer. The Courtauld Institute of Fine Arts has become involved, and in 1997 a bid for a lottery grant of £300,000 was made, to restore the paintings and carry out further excavations. Meanwhile the final restoration work was done on the tower.

Hundreds of visitors now come to see St Mary's. Bob Davey himself has been to Buckingham Palace, he has escorted Princess Margaret to the church, and he has received wild-flower seeds for the churchyard from Prince Charles's garden at Highgrove. But perhaps his greatest reward is the re-establishment of St Mary's as a living church. A service is now held there at least once a year, and if the weather is fine the worshippers fill the churchyard. The favourite hymn on these occasions is 'Come to the church in the wild wood …'

4 miles NE of North Walsham on the B1145

'A vision in carpentry' – and the heavenly host are quite impressive too

OPINIONS ABOUT THE ROOF OF St Peter and St Paul's vary – but only in degree. 'One of the finest double hammerbeam roofs in East Anglia,' says one gazetteer guardedly. 'The best double hammerbeam roof in Norfolk,' says another, more firmly. The church guide, understandably, goes a step further. 'This is probably the handsomest parish church roof in the country' – and after a page of eulogy it sums up decisively: 'A vision in carpentry'.

It is certainly quite a roof. Tradition has it that it never was intended for this little village, but was being carried on board ship to a more important destination when it was wrecked off the Norfolk coast. A more imaginative version suggests that it was actually the elaborately-carved hull of the ship itself, which survived intact and was turned upside-down by some enterprising builder to fit on the church. More likely, alas, the real explanation is that some of the timbers were salvaged from wrecks along the coast,

and the story just grew and grew …

Experts enthuse over the skill with which these timbers were put together, to create over two thousand square feet of intricate roofing. It has even been suggested that the effect would be better without the carved angels, to give an uninterrupted view of its elegance. But to the layman it is the angels that are the main attraction – and the prophets and apostles and saints who share the roof-space, a hundred and sixty of them altogether, poised in mid-air as if ready for flight. In the unlikely event of a dull sermon at Knapton, one imagines the congregation might spend their time, not counting sheep but the Heavenly Host.

The man responsible for all this was a sixteenth-century rector, who is said to have paid for it to be erected in 1503. His name was John Smith, and I have often commented that if he wanted to immortalize an otherwise unmemorable name, he certainly did it in style. Unfortunately the guidebook just mentions that he happened to be rector at the time, and leaves it at that.

It does give due credit, though, to the author of the ingenious Greek palindrome on the cover of the thirteenth-century font, another of the church's great treasures. Greek scholars can work out what it is from the English translation: 'Wash my sins and not my face only'. It is attributed to the Emperor Leo in about AD 900 – one of those Greeks who not only had a word for it, but had a word for it backwards too.

LEFT Just a few of the 160 prophets, apostles, saints and angels who share the two thousand square feet of carved roof-space.

5 miles N of Fakenham on the B1105

The church was gutted, the organ blown up, but the bells ding-donged merrily on high

ST MARY'S IS RATHER LIKE AN ecclesiastical Tardis. Outside it looks like a typical medieval Norfolk church, as familiar as Dr Who's police-box, but inside it is a modern church with new pillars and ceilings, new furnishings and decorations. It is the result of a fire in 1961 which completely gutted the building, but left the walls and windows (apart from the glass) intact. The interior was rebuilt within the old walls, to provide perhaps the best of both worlds.

The fire was not the only disaster to hit St Mary's. A century earlier the new organ was astonishingly blown up by gunpowder – on November 5th. It could hardly have been rated an Act of God. It is suspected the church musicians, who played for services before the organ arrived, decided to dispose of this newfangled device, just as the Luddites attacked the new machinery in the factories – but nothing was ever proved, and their efforts were equally unsuccessful. The present organ is so highly rated it has been used for recitals by the BBC .

Walsingham is best known, of course, as a place of pilgrimage, from the time the Virgin Mary appeared in a vision to the Saxon Lady of the Manor in 1061 and told her to build a replica there of her home in Nazareth. Even Henry VIII walked barefoot to the shrine – then had his famous change of heart, dissolved the abbey, closed the shrine and had Mary's statue burnt. But the parish church continued, and it was here that the restoration of the shrine took place in 1922. The vicar, Father Hope Patten, erected a replica of the original statue in the church, and it was the centre of pilgrimage until it was moved to a new shrine in the village. A small figure of Our Lady of Walsingham marks where it stood.

Throughout all the changes many features of St Mary's survived, notably the elaborate fifteenth-century font, carved with the Seven Sacraments, and a number of monuments. There are modern sculptures too, particularly in the south chapel, where there is also a tablet in memory of Dr George Ratcliffe Woodward, a nineteenth-century vicar who wrote, among many other carols, 'Ding dong merrily on high'. Or rather, he translated it from the French, though it is difficult to work out the first line in its original form. Could it really have been *'Ding dong heureusement en haut'*?

RIGHT These curtains are not for pulling – they are a modern sculpture.

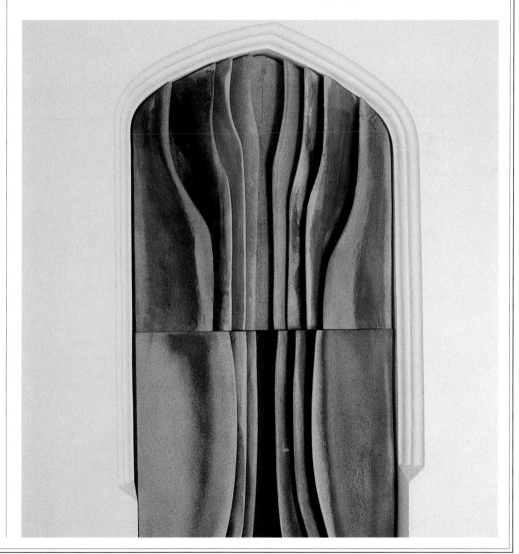

6 miles SE of Swaffham on the B1077

The organ is magnificent – but Pugin might look twice at that east window

THE ORGAN IS RARELY THE MOST outstanding feature of a country church, but All Saints' does have a remarkable one – if only at second hand. It came from nearby West Tofts church, which has been in a Ministry of Defence restricted training area since 1942, and can only be reached by special permit. Many of its furnishings were transferred to other Norfolk churches, and South Pickenham acquired the organ.

The instrument was part of a comprehensive restoration at West Tofts carried out in the last century by the renowned church architect Augustus Pugin. He died before it was finished, but he left detailed plans for the decorations and furniture, including the elaborate organ case, with wing doors like a triptych concealing the front pipes.

It is the paintings on these doors which make it so striking. They are splendid depictions of the Adoration of the Magi and the Nativity, the work of an Antwerp artist in 1856. And incidentally, the organ sounds pretty good too …

All Saints' was originally thatched, but in 1604 the entire roof was blown off in a violent storm, and it was replaced by one with a much lower pitch, covered in lead. However, the lofty east window was left intact, so its tracery projects about three feet above the roof and the wall, giving an oddly unfinished appearance to that end.

Inside, there is an interesting contrast between one or two of the memorials. When Piers Moreton of Pickenham Hall died in a road accident in 1967 at the age of twenty-one, his family gave the fine Jacobean pulpit in his memory; but when Edward Mills died a century earlier, he was buried just inside the door 'so that everyone entering the church walked on his grave', according to the church guide. Mr Mills it seems, was a very unpopular man. In the 1800s he lent money to the purchasers of the Hall, but twice repossessed the property when they could not keep up the payments. The debt was eventually paid, but public opinion was against him and when he died, this was how the villagers expressed it.

Thomas Turner, who died in 1822, seemed to have been unpopular in the village too, but according to his tombstone he did not care. The inscription begins: 'Adieu, vain world, I've had enough of thee, and careless am of what you think of me', and it ends: 'Your smiles I court not, nor your frown I fear. My time is gone, my head lies quiet here.'

People get along much better these days in South Pickenham …

LEFT The organ with its magnificent decorated doors was transferred from a church which is now in an Army restricted area.

8 miles E of Norwich on the B1140

Two quarrelling sisters
– or just a boundary change?

NOBODY REALLY KNOWS WHY these two churches share the same churchyard. There is a delightful legend about churches like this, where one has fallen derelict: that the Lord of the Manor divided his land equally between his two daughters, who quarrelled and built their own churches in the same churchyard, just to annoy each other. One was nice, the other was nasty, and it was the nasty sister's church that collapsed.

Unfortunately the original St Lawrence's Church was probably erected earlier than St Mary's, and it was there for five hundred years before being burnt out. Even then it was partially rebuilt, and only fell derelict after the last war – a long time for the nasty sister's nastiness to take effect. More likely St Lawrence's originally served the whole of the Manor, then part was hived off as a separate parish, and St Mary's was built in the same churchyard because it was already a sacred and consecrated site.

The fire at St Lawrence's was in 1827. The chancel was restored and enlarged, and continued to function with its own rector for sixty-odd years. At that stage a joint incumbent was appointed, but the parishes were not officially united until 1986. By then St Lawrence's had been derelict for years, but more recently it has been restored as a Centre for Training and the Arts. The site of the former nave is now a herb garden.

Meanwhile St Mary's has continued in use as the parish church. Its great treasure is the medieval rood screen, not only because of its paintings but its inscription, which must be unique. It is partly in Latin and partly in what is officially Middle English, but reads remarkably like broad Norfolk.

It starts in Latin, translating as 'Pray for the souls of John Galt and of his wives', then perhaps the writer could not think of the Latin for 'who have cause this screen to be painted', so he dropped into his native dialect: 'the qweche had doon peyntyn this perke'. In other words: 'the which had done painting this screen' – 'perke' was the Anglian word for 'screen'.

Now hent that a rum owld do, bor?

BELOW South Walsham's two churches share a churchyard. St Lawrence's, on the right, is now a Centre for Training and the Arts.

6 miles W of King's Lynn off the A17

This time it wasn't the Devil that detached the tower, just a far-sighted architect

THE DETACHED TOWER OF ST Clement's has a rather more logical explanation than the usual one favoured by romantics, that the Devil tried to steal it but his foot caught on the church roof. When the church was built in the fourteenth century on the old Norman and Saxon foundations, it was originally intended to erect the tower on top of the choir, between the chancel and the nave, and indeed there are four large arches there which look as if they ought to be supporting something. But when the architect redid his sums, he realised that the combined weight would probably make the whole building subside into the marshy soil below; it would be swallowed up in one enormous gulp.

Even without the tower, the west end of St Clement's started to sink, so the great buttresses had to be added. But the tower stood firm, and the villagers had particular reason to be grateful to that architect on two occasions in the seventeenth century, when the Wash broke down the sea-walls and flooded the area. They were able to dash straight into the tower and take refuge on top of it, with supplies being brought by boat from King's Lynn.

These days, thanks to land reclamation, the Wash is miles away, but when the church was built the Barnack stone was brought all the way to Terrington by boat. Indeed, when the villagers were blamed in 1600 for letting the church fall into disrepair, they said they spent all their available time and money maintaining the nearby sea-wall. Judging by the two subsequent floods, they might have done better concentrating on the church.

St Clement's great treasure is its sixteenth-century font cover, which opens up to show the baptism, fasting and temptation of Christ, in one magnificent panorama. Another quite unexpected find is in the south vestry, where there are two ancient figures of St Clement and St Christopher. Apparently they used to stand in niches on the outside of the west wall. They were found in 1887 lying behind two of the buttresses, perhaps hidden there during the Civil War. No doubt they were taken inside temporarily, and no one has yet got around to putting them back.

The great east window is dedicated to the men from the parish who failed to return from the 1914–18 War. It is a striking memorial, but as no fewer than one hundred men were lost from this only moderate-sized village, it deserves to be.

LEFT The sixteenth-century font case has a panorama of scenes from the life of Christ.

2 miles N of Acle off the B1140

The font is splendid, but the whalebone has a stranger tale to tell

AT ST MARGARET'S THEY SAY THE fourteenth-century font is 'probably the most beautiful ancient font in Norfolk', and they could well be right. It is covered in intricate carvings, from the wreath of foliage and strange animals on the pediment to the representation of the Two Sacraments on the plinth and the creatures of the Revelation on the bowl. But when you have sorted out which figures are which, and sympathized with the angels who are carrying the whole weight of the massive bowl on their backs, you can find a little light relief in two other items which are rather less common in churches than fonts are. One is a large, flat, metal dragon; the other is the rib-bone of a whale.

The dragon has the simpler history. It used to be the weathervane on the church tower until it became unsafe and was taken down in 1982. It is not one of St George's legendary opponents; St Margaret of Antioch had a nasty encounter with a dragon, and this is her church.

The whalebone is much more unlikely, since Upton has no connection with whaling and is quite a distance from the sea. Its story dates back to Christmas Day, 1612, when two local ne'er-do-wells, Wicked Will Enderton and Simon Bullock, 'did profanely and disorderly behave themselves', in the words of the contemporary archdeacon's report.

'In the tyme of evening prayer,' it said, 'they came into the parish church with a great whalebone upon their shoulders, and with ye birds, a robin redbreast and a wren, tied by a thread and hanging upon the said bone. Wicked Will was making a great and roaring noise all the way of his coming. They fell down as though heavily or grievously loaded' – as indeed they were, and not just by the whalebone – 'and the said Wicked Will in a wild, profane and lewd manner, knelt upon his knees and prayed for the priest, and for his wife, and for his great dog – to the dishonour of God Almighty.'

There the report ends, but no doubt the priest had them ejected and in due course some sort of punishment was imposed. Wicked Will and his friend disappeared into obscurity, but the whalebone – or is it just *a* whalebone? – survives in Upton Church.

BELOW The bier is for carrying bodies, but it makes a handy whalebone rest.

9 miles W of King's Lynn off the A17

The Queen of the Marshland is 'unbelievably special'; Tom Hickathrift is a bit unbelievable too

PRINCE CHARLES, A GREAT PATRON OF country churches, reckons St Peter's is one of the finest, certainly in Norfolk. 'The way the light floods in on the stone and the lined wood and the white-washed walls creates an unbelievably special combination,' he told me. The Archbishop of Brazil called it 'a place filled with holiness'. And any number of experts have praised the majesty and elegance of what is called locally the Queen of the Marshland.

To me it is all these things and more, because it also has a fascinating collection of ecclesiastical curiosities. They start in the porch, a pair of well-worn pattens hanging on the wall – wooden-soled sandals for sloshing through the Fenland mud before the invention of the gumboot. 'It is requested that all persons take off their pattens at the church door' says the equally well-worn notice below.

Inside, the curiosities continue. There is a wooden 'hude', a kind of portable sentry-box to put beside graves for the parson at rainy funerals; an ancient wooden rocking-cradle, now used for flowers instead of babies; a carved oak almsbox on top of a pole – perhaps the original 'pillar-box'; and a pair of ornamental crooks 'laid up' by the Victorian Marshland Shepherds Club, a pastoral equivalent of the Masons.

The font is so high that the parson has to balance rather precariously on a narrow stone step at baptisms; one false move and the baby could finish up inside it. There is a long-standing joke about Fenmen being born with webbed feet; this might be the first occasion they needed them. Reaching the pulpit requires a good sense of balance too: the stairs that wind up to it round a stone pillar have no protective railing. And the high altar really is high, reached by nine steps from the chancel, which itself is quite high. The reason is 'The Bolthole', an arched passage immediately underneath the altar, from one side of the church to the other. Some say it is an ancient right of way, but it seems more likely it was to enable processions to get round the church, which is right on the boundary wall.

Nearby on the church wall is the belligerent figure of Tom Hickathrift, the local giant-killer. He regularly delivered beer from Lynn to Wisbech, and it is said that one day a giant blocked his path. Incensed at the delay, Tom took the axle off his cart to use as a club, held a wheel in the other hand as a shield, and killed the giant. It was perhaps the earliest example of road-rage – and helped to provide one more fascinating curiosity at St Peter's.

LEFT 'The Bolthole' under the altar was either a processional route, and ancient right of way – or both.
RIGHT The interior of St Peter's: 'unbelievably special', says Prince Charles.

2 miles SE of Wells-next-the-Sea off the A149

Some of the stained glass is a jumble – but why are those women with the Pope?

FROM THE OUTSIDE ST MARY'S STILL looks medieval, like All Saints' at the other end of the village, but in 1800 the church register records that it was 'stripped for repair', and when it opened again fifteen months later it was a Georgian church inside, with a plaster ceiling, box pews, and a towering three-decker pulpit. It is still the same, with the wooden pegs for gentlemen's hats and a Georgian font with slender stem and shallow bowl, looking every inch a birdbath.

The man responsible was the Revd Wenman Henry Langton, a kinsman of the patron, Thomas Coke, later Earl of Leicester, and therefore well able to afford it. He was more economical, though, over his choice of stained-glass windows. He bought them second-hand from a Norwich dealer, John Hampp, and the fact that some of them did not match St Mary's windows did not deter him at all. Where necessary he split up scenes and figures into their separate parts to fit the available space.

It is said a later rector followed his lead and paid sixpence to any local boy who found a fragment of stained glass, so he could fill the remaining gaps. One wonders how many windows in neighbouring churches got broken in the process …

Some scenes, however, survived intact, notably in the south chancel

RIGHT The lofty three-decker pulpit towers over the box pews – and gives the parson a good view of the occupants.

window. Two of its panels clearly depict the Pope, surrounded by cardinals, archbishops, abbots holding their croziers of office – and abbesses, also with croziers. Canon Bill Sayer, the present rector, believes it represents the Council of Trent, when the Roman Catholic hierarchy met after the Reformation – and the presence of the abbesses is highly significant.

'You hear so much nonsense these days about women not being appreciated in the Church, and how they've been badly treated and undervalued,' he told me, 'and yet here in a small piece of stained glass in a Norfolk church it is all destroyed. Here are women exercising authority with episcopal jurisdiction, three or four hundred years ago, right at the very centre of the Church.'

So the old Continental stained glass might be taken as justifying the ordination of women, but Canon Sayer believes the opposite. Women's ministry, he says, is complementary to men's, neither better nor worse, but different.

Either way, how lucky that the Revd Werman Langton did not mix up those pieces with the rest of his stained-glass jigsaw!

RIGHT According to the rector, this window proves that 'women exercized authority with episcopal jurisdiction ... right at the very centre of the church.

St Andrew's, Wellingham

A mystery saint, and a puzzling Pile

St Andrew's is an unassuming little church in an unassuming little village, but it has a rood screen with some of the best-preserved medieval paintings in Norfolk. Cromwell's men did scratch some of the saints' faces – they even had a go at St George's horse – but after more than 450 years they are still pictures of rood health.

Most of the figures are easily identifiable, but one of them remains a mystery; the experts cannot agree. The saint is dressed in full armour, carrying a spear and a sword which is not unusual, but there is a tiny king spread-eagled at his feet, flat on his back with his crown still perched on his head.

An early church guide suggested it was St Oswald vanquishing King Penda. It was only when the Victorian pulpit was moved in the 1980s that the remains of the saint's name were revealed. There were just the first three letters, a capital 'M', then an 'a', then 'r' or 'u', with room for five or six more.

St Martin? St Maurice? St Maximus? None of them is particularly associated with small supine kings. The most ingenious suggestion was St Margaret of Antioch, who is sometimes represented in male clothing. She fell foul of a wicked governor, who fed her to a dragon, and when the dragon 'burst asunder' and she emerged, miraculously unscathed, he had her beheaded instead.

St Margaret is often pictured vanquishing the dragon. The theory was that the artist got the story wrong and put the

RIGHT St George slays the dragon, but loses face anyway – so does his horse.

Governor at her feet instead. But I think I have a better one. He could have been foretelling how a twentieth-century 'Blessed Margaret', Mrs Thatcher, spreadeagled the MP who coined that phrase, Norman St John Stevas, and sent him off to the Lords in a peer's coronet to get him out of the way.

St Andrew's has another little puzzle. The names on the war memorial are in alphabetical order, with one exception, Frederick Pile. I discovered why. Mr Pile was killed by a stray Zeppelin bomb while walking down the village street, and after the war the villagers were not sure if he qualified for inclusion on the memorial; he did not die on active service, but he was killed by enemy action. So they compromised: their only civilian casualty was included in the names, but Frederick is at the bottom of the pile…

3 miles S of Wells-next-the-Sea on the B1105

Why a Norfolk tower from Leeds is named after Ontario's state flower

ALL SAINTS' IS ONE OF THOSE NORFOLK country churches which make such an impact with their sheer size and spaciousness that it is easy to miss their odder little features. There is Wighton's Royal coat of arms, for instance, a common enough decoration, but this is the coat of arms of George IV, not the most popular of monarchs, and the lion and unicorn on each side, instead of standing in their usual supporting role, are creeping furtively on all fours, as if embarrassed to be there. The experts deduce that the artist, a Mr Godman, did not approve of the Hanoverian succession.

Then there is the touchingly inscribed tomb of Lady Elizabeth Bacon, who died in childbirth in 1686. Frustratingly it is in Latin, but it reads: 'Here lies Elizabeth, pious wife of Sir Robert Bacon, Baronet of Egmere, who died together with her new-born twins, whom she took away with her, one on either arm.' But there were six other children, and their descendants still live in Norfolk.

The windows in the side aisles are interesting, if you know your saints. The idea was to portray the Apostles, but there are more windows than Apostles, and anyway the artist wanted to skip Judas. So he replaced him with St Matthias, and St Paul and St Barnabas make up the numbers.

Wighton's most unusual feature, though, is its tower. It looks an average medieval tower at first glance, but it is only twenty

years old. Its predecessor collapsed in 1965, and lay in ruins until Mr Leeds Richardson turned up, ten years later, from Ontario in Canada, in search of his ancestors. Happily he found a couple buried in the churchyard, so to celebrate he presented the church with a hundred thousand dollars to rebuild the tower. In addition, he paid for a set of bells

to be hung inside the newly-named Trillium Tower.

So All Saints' must be the envy of other country churches waiting for enough money for their own rebuilding projects. Instead of 'Why are we waiting?' they may well be murmuring, 'Why aren't we Wighton?'

RIGHT Lady Elizabeth Bacon died with her new-born twins: 'she bore them away with her, one on either arm.'

7 miles N of Great Yarmouth on the B1159

Fishermen's Corner, Falstaff's Porch
– and bells with an extra long boi-oing

THE CHURCH OF THE HOLY TRINITY and All Saints is an unusual pairing, and there is no record of it coming in two stages, like many double dedications. A medieval inscription over the entrance announces firmly: 'In Honore Sancte Trinitatis et Omnium Sanctorum', so the full dedication has existed since the church was built.

The porch itself, weather-beaten but still imposing, is believed to have been paid for by Sir John Fastolf, the wealthy Norfolk warrior-knight on whom Shakespeare probably based his Falstaff. His arms may have been on one of the shields which the two carved angels are carrying, but they have been worn away by five centuries of coastal gales and storms. It has also lost the figures which used to stand on the parapet, but those on the battlements of the tower, 130 feet higher, have surprisingly survived, an assortment of strange animals and naked men ('not frozen tourists', adds the guidebook with a welcome flash of humour).

The ring of six bells insides the tower have a unique feature which few visitors are aware of – unless they have a good ear for a bell-note. The bells were cast a century ago in the little village foundry at Redenhall, in South Norfolk, and they are fitted with the Patent Redenhall Clapper. It is a remarkable device which allows the ball on the clapper to slide down the stem as soon as it strikes the bell. The result, so it is claimed, is to make the bells resound much longer; in

RIGHT Fishermen's Corner, in memory of fatalities at sea, was created by a rector who himself died rescuing a drowning choirboy.

other words, instead of going 'Boing!' it goes 'Boi-oi-oing …'

To mariners, however, the tower is valued more as a navigation mark than for the sounds that come out of it. Unfortunately it has not always been enough to save them in the storms that sweep this coast, and the church contains a unique memorial to the local men who have died at sea. Fishermen's Corner, in the north-west corner of the nave, was set up in 1927 by the rector, the Revd Clarence Porter, who filled it with

various items connected with the sea; even the Crucifix is made from ships' timbers.

On the wall nearby is perhaps the saddest memorial, to Father Porter himself who died while rescuing a choirboy from drowning, five years later. He got the lad safely to shore, but suffered a heart attack on the beach. He was forty-seven. When his memorial was dedicated the lad he saved, Douglas George, was in the congregation, and members of his family still cherish Father Porter's memory.

3 miles NE of Sudbury off the B1115

Two kinds of brass: Sir Robert's gets rubbed, William Jennens hoarded his

THE FOURTEENTH-CENTURY BRASS of Sir Robert de Bures in All Saints' is so famous – 'perhaps the finest and most beautiful figure of the cross-legged period', as one expert cryptically described it – that a copy has been installed beside it so brass-rubbers don't wear out the original. Sir Robert faithfully served Edward I and II, and was handsomely rewarded: Acton was one of his manors.

His was a standard story of the times, but the tales behind other features of Acton church range from the bizarre to the macabre – from the unexploded Zeppelin bomb preserved inside the tower, to the murderer who was surreptitiously interred in the chancel. Charles Drew was convicted and hanged for killing his father and would normally have been buried in unconsecrated ground, but the vicar happened to be his brother-in-law.

The strangest of the tales at All Saints' is linked with the massive tomb of Robert Jennens; his son William (who was too mean to have a tomb) was the notorious Miser of Acton. He augmented the family fortune by visiting the gaming tables in London, not to gamble but to lend money to the gamblers. For every pound he loaned in the evening, he got back a guinea next day – a swift profit of five per cent.

He rarely spent any of it, and his only friends were his dogs. He always took an old setter to London with him, but on his last visit, it is said, he inexplicably left it behind.

RIGHT The elaborate monument to Robert Jennes. His son, the Miser of Acton, was too mean – or modest? – to have one.

The dog set out after him, and three days later was found lying exhausted and dying on the steps of his house in Grosvenor Square – where William Jennens lay dying too.

The Acton Miser had no close relations and left no will. There were many rival claimants, and the lawsuits lasted for years until the estate eventually went to a distant cousin, Earl Howe. It is said to have inspired Charles Dickens to write *Bleak House*: his fictional case of Jarndyce and Jarndyce could have been based on Jennens and Jennens – and Howe!

7 miles NW of Saxmundham off the A1120

Watch out for the sundial, mind the slope – and be sure to look under the bed

THE FIRST FEATURE THAT STRIKES YOU about St John's Church – and it actually looks as if it is about to – is the sundial over the porch. It is set apparently askew, with one corner jutting over the parapet. The reason is that the church itself is out of alignment: instead of the east end being at the east, it is in fact at the north-east.

This is not just a misjudgement on the part of the architect. Legend has it that the reason goes back to pre-Christian days. The church was built on a pagan holy site, from the time when midsummer was celebrated at Badingham with great bonfires, and the church was dedicated to St John the Baptist because his feast is celebrated on midsummer day. So the masons built it to make sure that on its patronal festival the rising sun would shine directly through the 'east' window – the Christian equivalent of those pagan fires.

Nobody is quite sure how they managed it so accurately. One theory is that they went by a stone circle which stood on the site. Presumably the early sun-worshippers waited until midsummer morning with their stones poised, then set them up to frame the sun's rays. Whatever system they used, it works; but it does cause a little nervousness, walking under that out-of-kilter sundial.

The other obvious peculiarity of St John's is its slope. It is quite a climb from the west end of the nave – or rather, the south-west end – to the chancel. Needless to say, there is a theory about this too, which seems almost as unlikely as the instantly-positioned stone circle. When the church was built there was a great fear of the Plague, and

it was given a slope because that made it easier to swab out after services: the water just ran down the aisle and out of the door.

In this church of curious legends, it is comforting to find a more familiar set of pictures on the fifteenth-century font. The panels depict the Seven Sacraments, from baptism to the Extreme Unction, and they are reckoned to be among the finest of their kind in the country. But in St John's, even the Seven Sacraments have a slightly eccen-

tric twist, because the stonemason obviously had an eye for realism. On the final panel the dying patient is receiving the last rites, surrounded by his grieving relatives. But one's eye is drawn downwards. Could this be the only font in England, one wonders, which depicts under the death-bed a pair of slippers and a medieval potty?

BELOW AND RIGHT A crooked sundial on the porch, and a practical potty on the font.

5 miles N of Lowestoft off the A12

No, you won't find David Copperfield's grave
– but don't tell the tourists

BLUNDESTON HAS NEVER REALLY recovered from being selected by Charles Dickens as the birthplace and first home of David Copperfield. So many visitors from abroad come to look for the features mentioned in the opening chapters that Blundeston has decided, if you can't beat 'em, join 'em, and the village sign depicts Copperfield as a boy, looking at the church – the main centre of pilgrimage.

Unfortunately there is not much Copperfield memorabilia to see. You can guess at which pew he sat in with Peggotty, where she could see their house through the window 'to make as sure as she can that it's not being robbed, or is not in flames'. And the churchyard is still much as he describes it: 'There is nothing half so green as the grass of that churchyard; nothing half so shady as its trees; nothing half so quiet as its tombstones'. But the sundial he admired on the porch has been replaced, and search as you may, you won't find his grave.

There is one worth finding, though, because of its unique anti-leapfrog device. When the local schoolmaster, George Fisk, died in 1835 he asked for three spikes to be set into his headstone to prevent his pupils jumping over it. Only one spike survives, and the hedge has grown so close that it would be difficult anyway – but it is the thought that counts.

Inside the church the Norman font was originally square, but had its corners cut off in the fifteenth century to make it fashionably octagonal. The 'houselling benches', used in medieval times before the introduction of Communion rails – 'housel' was the old word for the Eucharist – are in fact copies made in 1928. But one feature of St Mary's has been unchanged for many centuries, its unusual version of a leper's squint.

It is a small round opening in the west wall. Looking from outside through the long circular hole, the altar at the far end of the church is so distant that it seems you are viewing it though the wrong end of a telescope. So could it really have been used by lepers?

'Its original purpose remains a matter for debate,' says the church leaflet. But it might be worth suggesting to tourists that David Copperfield used to peep through it if he was late for a service, to see if Peggotty was yet in her pew.

RIGHT This schoolmaster's tombstone has a device to stop his pupils jumping over it. Leapfrog would be particularly uncomfortable.

3 miles N of Woodbridge off the A12 (near Bredfield)

Shoes and socks off in the pulpit
– 'All Fitzgeralds are mad, but John is the maddest …'

THIS IS NOT AN EASY CHURCH TO find, because Boulge is just a couple of farms and a few cottages scattered round what used to be a park. But pilgrims beat a path here from all over the world to visit the grave of Edward Fitzgerald, translator of the *Rubaiyat of Omar Khayyam*, and brother of the nineteenth-century squire and rector, John Purcell Fitzgerald of Boulge Hall.

Edward was a known eccentric, but his brother could be odder. Edward once observed: 'All Fitzgeralds are mad, but John is the maddest of all – because he doesn't know it!' He was also probably the wealthier, and in the 1860s he completely restored and enlarged St Michael and All Angels. The Fitzgerald aisle is full of his family's memorials, and there is a stained-glass window in memory of John himself, but his real memorial – as has been said of other church builders – is all around you.

Having rebuilt the church, he made good use of it. His sermons could last for a couple of hours, and he was known to remove his shoes and socks in the pulpit to keep himself cool. He would also take a candle from the bracket beside him and wave it vigorously to emphasize a point – and to ensure, perhaps, that his flagging parishioners stayed awake. It also meant that when he waxed eloquent, he could also wax the front row of the congregation.

However, the candles must have been a boon, because the newly-installed stained glass cut out much of the light: 'the church

is bathed in devotional dusk', as the guidebook elegantly puts it. Do try to see the massive Norman font, which is plain and uncarved but nevertheless of great rarity. It is made of blue-black Tournai marble from Belgium, one of only ten in England. The worn corners of the bowl show how it becomes black and shiny if it is rubbed.

The Fitzgerald mausoleum in the churchyard looks in rather a sorry state under its covering of brambles, but Edward is wisely buried beside it. At the head of his simple grave is a rose tree, grown from seed taken from a tree beside Omar Khayyam's grave in what was then Persia. It looked a little sad when I saw it, perhaps because so many people take cuttings, but it manages to bloom twice a year – once, it is said, for Edward Fitzgerald, and once for Omar Khayyam.

RIGHT Edward Fitzgerald's grave has Omar Khayyam's rose tree at its head.

4 miles SW of Diss off the A143

Many of its earlier treasures were lost, but Billy and Harry will live on

ST MARY'S HAS SUFFERED EXTENSIVELY over the centuries. Its chancel screen was broken down 'with axes and hammers', and parts of it were used later to make the pulpit. The famous Cross of Burgate was also destroyed; no one is sure why it was famous, but 'pious associations were attached to it and many ancient wills left bequests to it', says the venerable brochure. The medieval altar tomb of Sir William de Burgate, and the font which bears his arms, have somehow survived, but the ancient altar was broken – a piece of it lies under the present one. Windows were smashed, pew-ends defaced, rubbish dumped in the tower, 'which ragged curtains strove to conceal'. It reached the stage when a farm labourer commented: 'What's the use o' that owd place? It would make a good bullock shed.'

Happily St Mary's has been comprehensively restored, and the Revd B. Appleyard, a rector who served as a chaplain in the First World War, added some distinctive touches. It was his idea to turn the former Easter sepulchre, which was occupied by the organ blower, into a war shrine. It contains the chalice and paten he used in France and his old tin hat. Other items, like the candle-holders made from shell-cases, were the work of soldier-craftsmen who were patients at the casualty station in Belgium where he was chaplain.

During the 1920s two new boys joined the choir who went on to make a lifetime contribution to St Mary's, and they have been recognized in an unusual way. Harry Baker, now eighty-three, and his friend Billy Garrod, two years younger, pumped the organ, rang the bells, raised money, and served as churchwardens until a year or two ago. Billy was a lay elder for fourteen years, Harry still grows plants and flowers to sell for the church.

In 1995 they were immortalized in stone: their carved heads were installed in the porch on each side of the door. They both told me the carvings reminded them of their mothers, and I can understand why, because they are portrayed wearing tight-fitting flat hats and a wimple tied under the chin, rather like medieval matrons. Perhaps it was to make them look more in keeping with their fourteenth-century surroundings. But there is no mistaking who they are, from Harry's bushy eyebrows to Billy's firm chin.

It is the sort of accolade only accorded these days to bishops and royalty, and I am sure the old labourer who reckoned the church had become more like a bullock shed would be glad to know that, after its restoration, two old farmworkers are permanently guarding its door.

LEFT AND RIGHT Harry Baker and Billy West, forever guarding the church door. OPPOSITE The war shrine has candleholders made from shell cases.

7 miles NW of Saxmundham on the A1120

The sciapod is still sheltering under its foot: nobody told it about sunshades

S T MARY'S, SAYS ONE KNOWLEDGEABLE writer, is a church not to be missed 'even by the architecturally incurious'. Certainly it has other features which I am more curious about than its architecture, notably its unique sciapod, a creature which cannot be found, it is said, in any other church in the country. The sciapod was a legendary character who lived in hotter climes and developed one enormous foot as protection from the midday sun. He just lay on his back and held up his foot. Then presumably someone invented the sunshade, and the sciapod became extinct; it only survives in the form of a carved pew-end in St Mary's.

The church is reputed to have been built on the site of a Druid temple, where perhaps the sciapod would have had a special significance, in view of the Druids' interest in the sun. The other carvings on the pew-ends are equally impressive, if less unusual. The fine craftsmanship in St Mary's includes the sixteenth-century altar with a canopy for the pyx, made from one piece of wood, and the two screens protecting the north and south chapels.

In the Bardolph Chapel is the tomb of Lord Bardolph, one of the 'happy few' who fought alongside Henry V at Agincourt. He lies with his feet resting on a convenient eagle. His wife, who lies beside him, has a foot-rest which could either be a very small dragon or a very ferocious dog. The effigies were originally painted and believed to be of stone; in

RIGHT The last sciapod in England is still performing acrobatics to shelter from the sun.

fairly recent years the paint was cleaned off and they were found to be alabaster.

The list of rectors of St Mary's includes John Colet, who founded St Paul's School in 1512, and perhaps appropriately the church has on display a venerable teaching device. In the days before blackboards and pencil erasers, let alone magnetized iron filings, children learned to write and draw on another kind of reusable surface, a sand-table. If they got anything wrong, they could smooth out the sand and start again.

I tried it – and it still works.

In spite of its carvings and monuments, not everything in St Mary's has delighted the experts. When Dr M. R. Jones, the Provost of Eton, visited the church in the 1920s, he was not at all impressed by the windows. 'The old glass, not inconsiderable in amount, is decorative only, without pictures. The modern glazing is absolutely vile!'

Perhaps it is better to be 'architecturally incurious' …

10 miles NE of Ipswich off the B1069

The wood-carving rector found an unlikely use for a bed-head: he put it in the roof

ALL SAINTS' DOES NOT LOOK ITS BEST from the outside, as the guidebook freely admits. 'We have no magnificent profile, no tower – thank goodness … We are no more than a barn …' But it is still a fascinating church inside, if only because of the unique fifteenth-century church key on display, the tongue of which spells the old name of the village, IKE. However, the most striking attraction of All Saints' is its woodwork, mostly carved by one of the three generations of Darlings who have been rectors for nearly a hundred of the last hundred and fifty years.

The earliest, 'Grandfather' Darling, is commemorated by the Victorian east window, which symbolizes the Barnardo children he brought to the village. There is a lion to represent St Mark, and some say its face is very like Grandfather's.

But it was his son, Archdeacon Darling, who made the greatest impact on the appearance of the church. His carvings range from the pulpit – in memory of his sister – to the pew ends in the chancel, quite a menagerie of exotic and homely creatures. He included his pet Irish setter, an owl that nested in one of his sheds, and an upright whelk-shell with two snails at its base, to form an unorthodox – and somewhat ambiguous – poppy-head. He also carved a polar bear and a penguin, not to reflect the severity of the Suffolk winter but to honour Captain Scott's ill-fated Antarctic expedition, which was very much in people's mind at the time.

RIGHT The penguin symbolizes an Antarctic expedition, not a Suffolk winter.

The archdeacon's most unusual contribution to the woodwork in the church was not exactly his own work. The story goes that he was visiting a sick parishioner and greatly admired his oak bed-head, carved with an angel with outstretched wings. Presumably a few gentle hints were dropped, and in due course the bed-head was presented to the church. Somehow he acquired seven more identical panels – or could he have copied the pattern himself? – and they now provide a fitting decoration in the church roof.

So do not be deterred by the lack of a tower or a magnificent profile; All Saints' is quite a Darling church.

10 miles W of Saxmundham on the B1119

Good news and bad news for the Howards – and a gap that remained unfilled

THE CHANCEL OR ST MICHAEL'S is a little wider, and a lot grander, than the nave, thanks to Thomas Howard, third Duke of Norfolk. He built it to accommodate the family tombs of future Howards, and completed it just in time for his own to be included. He could easily have missed the boat; he was sentenced to death six years earlier, but Henry VIII died on the night before his execution was due, and he was reprieved. He is depicted on his tomb alongside his wife, and his collar is inscribed, almost indecipherably, with the grateful message: 'By the Grace of God, I am what I am.'

That reprieve was the good news for the duke. The bad news was that his son Henry was also due to be executed, but on the day before the king died; it was duly carried out. Henry and his wife have a much more colourful tomb than his father's, but instead of a grateful message round his collar, his coronet has been removed and placed beside him, to symbolize his execution. The mason was not tasteless enough to remove his actual head.

These two Howards were not the only ones to fall foul of their monarch. The fourth duke was executed for his friendship with Mary, Queen of Scots, by Queen Elizabeth I. He does not feature on a tomb, but his two wives, who died before him, lie side by side in the chancel – with a gap in between. He may have planned it for his next wife, on the assumption that she would die young too, but he never married again. Perhaps the news of that vacant space had reached the eligible ladies at Court and the message went round – a message famil-iar to City workers who use Bank Station – 'Mind the Gap' …

There are other striking features of Framlingham church which catch the eye, like the famous seventeenth-century organ at the far end, and the splendid 'Glory' behind the altar. But it is more difficult to spot the Flodden Helmet, perched on a bracket high up under the chancel roof. It was the second Duke of Norfolk's, who defeated the Scots at the Battle of Flodden in 1513 and stopped them from taking Henry VIII's throne. If he had know how the king was going to treat his descendants, he might not have bothered.

BELOW Henry Howard lost his head; the displaced coronet is a permanent reminder.

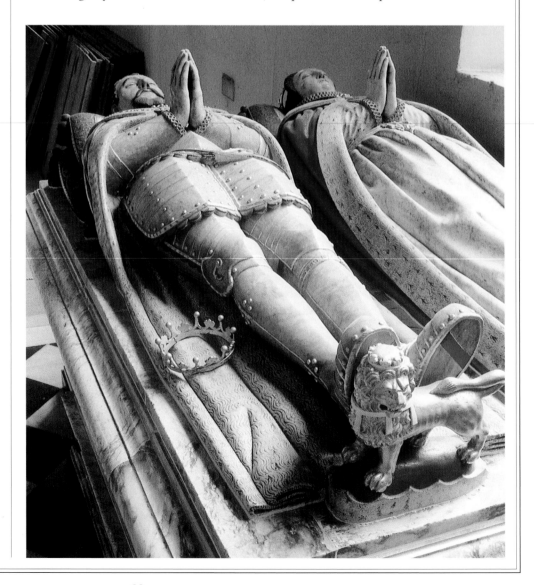

9 miles E of Bury St Edmunds off the A14

Medieval magicians with a secret lock, a one-card trick, and a swopped head

THE MEDIEVAL CRAFTSMEN WHO worked in St Ethelbert's Church liked to leave little puzzles for later generations, and one or two have proved highly successful. One example is the massive ironbound parish chest, which has the standard three locks – one opened by the vicar, the others by the churchwardens – but when the three keys are turned, the chest remains locked. There is in fact a hole in the side which takes a fourth 'key', a long rod which completes the process. It baffled the Puritans, and indeed it was only discovered earlier this century. Inside were some rare fifteenth-century treasures which were only saved by that locksmith's ingenuity.

One of the elaborate wall-paintings also proved puzzling – to me, at least. It shows Christ of the Trades, surrounded by various tools and implements. Among the hammers and pliers and saws there is a playing card, the six of diamonds, and I could only think that the artist was a poker player who completed a winning hand with a six of diamonds and decided to record it for posterity. However, I have been told by one expert that it represents the card-making trade – and by another that it was one of the activities prohibited on Sundays. Nice to know even the experts are in two minds.

The two-storey vestry, unusual in itself, has caused similar debates. Did it accommodate a hermit, or was it a chantry chapel? The upper floor was added later than the room below – by John and Katrynne Hoo, a surname with much scope for further confusion – so earlier hermits must have been rather cramped.

The most fascinating puzzle is the central section of the east window in the south aisle. It is apparently a bishop with four children, one of whom is holding what looks like a hockey-stick. In fact it is not a bishop at all. The head and shoulders were added to the body of St Mary Cleophas, and the four children are her saintly sons. The 'hockey-stick' is held by St James the Less, and it is actually a fuller's club, normally used for cleaning cloth but in his case for beating him to a martyr's death.

It is all very logical, once the switched heads have been explained, but it is bad news for hockey enthusiasts: they don't have a patron saint at Hessett after all.

RIGHT The switched head has caused some confusion. The 'bishop' is actually St Mary Cleophas with her saintly sons – who do not play hockey.

9 miles SW of Diss off the A143

The Rutherford windows should compensate for the Gotch it hasn't got

FROM A VISITOR'S VIEWPOINT, St Mary's suffers from two disadvantages. First, its most unusual treasure, a bell-ringer's beer pitcher known locally as the Gotch, is no longer on view in the church; a Bury St Edmunds museum has got the Gotch on permanent loan. It is a splendid piece of early eighteenth-century pottery, which can hold about two gallons of beer – that works out at two or three pints per bell-ringer. It was presented by an ex-ringer called Sam Moss, who obviously found ringing was thirsty work. It is inscribed: 'From London I was sent, as plainly does appear. It was with this intent, to be filled with strong beer. Pray remember the pitcher when empty.' These days, sadly, it can only be seen in Hinderclay on the village sign; the ringers are probably quite sad about it too.

St Mary's other disadvantage is its neighbours. The church is almost dwarfed by the very large and singularly unscenic agricultural buildings on the adjoining land. One day perhaps the trees will grow tall enough and thick enough to conceal them, but at present they do nothing to enhance the church's setting.

Perhaps to counter this, a former rector living in Hinderclay has been filling the windows on that side of the church with stained glass. The designs are modern, like the farm buildings, but they look a lot more attractive. They were created by the Revd John Rutherford's sister Rosemary, and he helped in her workshop. When she died he continued to install windows in her memory. There are paintings in the church too, which he provided. He recalls that during his incumbency in the seventies and eighties, the bishop encouraged him to brighten the church with pictures, and he has done so in more ways than one.

So never mind the church's looming neighbour, and the Gotch it hasn't got. It does have the Rutherford windows – and whether or not you like modern stained glass in ancient country churches, they do brighten up the place no end.

LEFT An example of the modern windows installed by a former Rector in memory of his sister – and to improve the view.

6 miles SW of Halesworth off the B1117

The rector's wife who lay on her back for years to paint the church roof

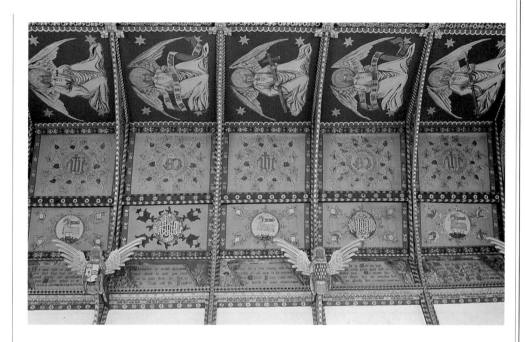

HUNTINGFIELD MIGHT INDEED have been one, to judge by the number of hounds which decorate St Mary's. There are greyhounds seated on pew-ends in the chancel, hounds' heads on outside window-frames, more greyhounds on a family vault in the churchyard, and another couple on a hatchment in the north aisle. The hatchment gives the clue to the canine connection, because it bears the arms of the Vanneck family, who were Lords of the Manor for two hundred years, and their arms are supported by two collared greyhounds. It is the Vanneck pew in the chancel, and the Vanneck vault outside.

The most remarkable feature of St Mary's, however, is its painted roof, not only for its brilliant colours but because of the person who painted it. Mildred Holland was the wife of a nineteenth-century rector, and in 1859 he closed the church for eight months so she could paint the chancel roof. Three years later, when she had got her breath back, she started on the roof of the nave, and it was not until 1886 that the rector was able to write, with some relief: 'Scaffolding finally taken down.' No doubt his parishioners were relieved too, to get their church back.

Apart from having the scaffolding erected and the roofs prepared for painting, the redoubtable Mrs Holland worked entirely unaided. It is said that she was hauled up the scaffolding on a stretcher, and painted the roofs while lying on her back – angels,

RIGHT The font cover given by a former Rector in memory of his wife, who painted the church roof.

ABOVE Some of the detailed work of Mrs Mildred Holland, as she lay on her back on the scaffolding.

banners, crowns, shields, the lot, and all in the greatest detail. These days the sight of a woman working in this way would hardly raise an eyebrow, but for a Victorian lady no longer in the first flush of youth, accustomed to wearing tight corsets and multi-layered petticoats, it must have seemed unconventional, to say the least.

She died before her husband, and he gave the font cover and the brass lectern in her memory. He had already paid for the restoration of the church, and for Mrs Holland's painting materials, which included over two hundred books of gold leaf. He also spent the best part of four years viewing his wife from below. That painted roof must be his memorial too.

St Mary's, Lakenheath

6 miles SW of Brandon on the B1112

A fortunate fall, a gullible tigress
– and the tussocks that led to the hassock

LAKENHEATH, TO MOST PEOPLE IN East Anglia, means the enormous American air base which has caused certain controversy over the years, though things are quieter now. But there was a Lakenheath village long before that, and St Mary's dates back to the Normans. However, even its own early version of low-flying aircraft, the angels in the roof, have proved unpopular in some quarters: they still bear the scars from Cromwell's soldiers. The church had rather better treatment from a much later general: Earl Kitchener lived in the village and was a benefactor. He has a memorial tablet in the north aisle.

Medieval wall-paintings were rediscovered early this century by a fortunate accident. A workman renewing the lime-wash on the walls fell off his ladder, and in falling he scraped off some of the limewash, revealing the paintings underneath. The story has a romantic angle too. It seem the workman, a Mr Olley, was busy up his ladder when a lady parishioner, a Miss Ward, came into the church and called up to him, 'Mr Olley, mind you don't fall.' Mr Olley gallantly replied: 'Miss Ward, I could fall for you' – and he did, in every sense. He was unhurt and they lived happily ever after.

St Mary's is also noted for its eccentric pew-ends, some of which have caused much discussion over the years. One of them, for instance, is officially called 'The Contortionist', but it could be interpreted quite differently. The most fascinating has been variously described as a dog licking out a frying-pan, or a tiger learning the banjo. The official theory is that it comes from a medieval manual on how to steal a tiger-cub from its mother, without her knowing it has gone. The idea was to place a mirror where the cub used to be, so the tigress looked at it, saw herself, and thought she was still looking at her cub. Somehow it hardly seems entirely foolproof.

Also in St Mary's are a couple of clumps of matted sedge, which could have quite an historical significance. They were dug out of the nearby fens by enterprising worshippers on their way to church, so they could kneel on them during prayers, instead of on the stone floor. These tussocks were the forerunners of what we call hassocks today.

LEFT A dog licking a frying-pan, or a tiger learning to play the banjo? Actually it shows how to use a mirror to steal a tiger cub …

3 miles SE of Bury St Edmunds off the A14

Who took the coat of arms off its beam?
And was it restored – or copied?

THE MOST EYE-CATCHING FEATURE in St Nicholas's Church is the huge coat of arms on the beam across the chancel; and probably the most eye-catching feature of the coat of arms is the greyhound, standing ostentatiously on its hind legs.

This is the coat of arms of Henry VIII, and it is believed to be the only one of its kind in any English church. It should therefore be of considerable value, but a slight doubt hangs over this because, according to a church historian, it was missing for a time during the last century. Nobody knows who took it, or why. Was it just to restore it, or to copy and replace it? And of course there was Colonel Rushbrooke …

At the time of its disappearance, the colonel was Lord of the Manor. When his family acquired the title they claimed to be descendants of the de Rushbrooks who held the village after the Norman Conquest, and they were returning after seven hundred years. Colonel Rushbrooke was a talented wood-carver, and he carved and installed the pews which face each other, collegiate-style, across the nave. He also carved the screen at the back of the church and the organ case above it, but unfortunately omitted to add an organ, and they still make do with an harmonium. It was his experience with carved wood that prompted a certain amount of speculation about the coat of arms. He would certainly have known the value of the original; and he would probably have had the skill to copy it.

RIGHT A rare Henry VIII coat of arms – but was it restored, or is it a copy?

The Jermyns, who were squires of Rushbrooke for four centuries, made more impact on the church than Colonel Rushbrooke. Thomas Jermyn rebuilt it in 1540, another Thomas gave the Communion table, and Henry Jermyn returned from exile in France after the Civil War with the Communion plate. As a Knight of the Garter he also acquired a 1662 Prayer Book bearing the name of a verger of St George's Chapel, Windsor, though why the verger had it, and how he got it from the verger, is not explained.

The most touching reminder of the Jermyns, among their many monuments, is a row of stones recording the deaths as babies of six children of the last Sir Thomas. Saddest of all is the memorial to the only son who grew up into boyhood. He died in 1692 in a boating accident, aged fifteen, the last of the family line – 'a day never to be forgotten by his unhappy father and mother'.

11 miles E of Bury St Edmunds off the A14

Could the green children be linked with the legend of the lectern?

WOOLPIT GETS ITS NAME FROM wolves, not wool, but there were indeed plenty of pits at Woolpit, and two of them achieved considerable fame, though for very different reasons. One is Lady's Well, a holy well reputed to have healing properties for eye complaints, and for once these claims have scientific confirmation. The water has been tested, and contains a higher percentage of sulphates, which are beneficial to the eyes, than any other water in the region.

Pilgrims came from all over Europe, and although the well is some way from the church, St Mary's had a chapel dedicated to Our Lady of Woolpit. The chapel has long since gone, but the wealth it must have attracted from the pilgrims may well have helped to provide the magnificent hammerbeam roof, with its two hundred angels and other carvings, and the elaborate porch – ' perhaps the most sumptuous in Suffolk', says one expert.

The other famous hole is the one through which the legendary Green Children emerged from their subterranean world, attracted by the sound of church bells. Their complexion was green, they only ate green vegetables, and they spoke a strange tongue. Sceptics say they were just vegetarians with understandably queasy stomachs who had strayed from another village with a different dialect, but the legend still persists. However, if you come across a stout metal cage over a grave in the churchyard, do not assume it is there to prevent any more Green Children emerging: it was just to protect it from grave-robbers.

There is another legend attached to the splendid brass lectern in the church, quoted by no less than a former Provost of Eton, Dr M. R. James. 'The eagle lectern,' he wrote, 'is old and good. It is said to have a trapdoor in the tail to extract contributions put in at the beak.'

The beak will indeed take a coin, and although there is no trapdoor at the rear, there is certainly a slit similar to those which return coins from slot-machines. But alas, I have tried it, and there seems to be no connection between the two. Maybe the story originated for the benefit of the Green Children – because you had to be pretty green to believe it!

RIGHT The eagle lectern could also be an offertory box – so the story goes.

1 mile S of Cobham on the A245

Famous brasses, a collection box for the Crusades – and Joanna Sturdy's bell

THE BEST WAY TO APPROACH STOKE D'Abernon is from the south, to avoid Cobham's suburban sprawl, and the most unspoilt part of St Mary's is on its south side too, where its oldest wall survives. It is said to date back to the late seventh century, soon after St Augustine arrived, making St Mary's one of the oldest churches in the country.

To the untutored eye, however, its most venerable feature is not the south wall but the parish chest, which not only held vestments but collected money for the Crusades. It has a slot in the lid and a receptacle inside. Every church was supposed to have one in 1199, by order of Richard I, but very few still have one today.

However, the devoted antiquarian is probably more interested in the brasses, claimed to be the oldest in the country, particularly the 1277 brass of Sir John D'Abernon and another of his son, fifty years later. There are brasses of the Norburys too, one showing Dame Anna Norbury with her four sons and four daughters in the folds of her robes. There are many of these treasures in the Norbury Chapel, built by Sir John Norbury to celebrate the victory at Bosworth Field over Richard III, in which he played a part. But, again for the uninitiated, the chapel's more unexpected feature is its fireplace, a rare luxury in pre-Reformation days, though Victorian squires and vicars had no hesitation in installing them for their own comfort. In this case it was perhaps because

RIGHT Joanna Sturdy's bell – the start of a sex revolution among the bell-founders?

the chapel was also used as a school.

But perhaps the most unusual feature of St Mary's is not immediately visible to the visitor, expert or not. One of the six bells in the tower was cast in about 1450. It is still as sound as – yes, a bell. And it was cast by a woman.

Her name was Joanna Sturdy, and I have commented in the past that if she was able to cope with the manual effort involved in casting bells, as well as the male prejudice that must have existed in such a man's

world as a medieval bell foundry, then Joanna was very sturdy indeed. Has the name perhaps been misspelt over the years? But do not breathe of such doubts in Stoke D'Abernon. The deeply-researched and well-authenticated church guide states firmly that the bell was cast by 'the famous woman bell-founder of Old Croydon'. So we can safely assume that Croydon, for all its unromantic associations today, saw the beginning of the bell-founders' sex revolution …

7 miles S of Chichester on the B2145

The church that moved two miles
– but left its chancel behind

ST PETER'S IS PROBABLY THE ONLY church in the country which manages to be in two places at once. The main body of the church – with a new chancel – is in Selsey; its original chancel is two miles north at Church Norton.

Until the middle of the last century it was all at Church Norton, where its origins go back to St Wilfrid, first Bishop of Selsey in the seventh century. He established himself on this windswept site, and Kipling's poem 'Eddi's Service' is based on Wilfrid's chaplain, Eddius Stephanus, who – according to Kipling – held a midnight service there on Christmas Eve, but only the animals turned up.

In the 1860s the rector, Prebendary Henry Foster, had similar problems persuading some of his flock to attend, because by then most of them lived in Selsey and there was some reluctance to make the two-mile journey to the church. So he decided – very unselfishly, since he lived in Church Norton himself – to move the church to Selsey. The Lady of the Manor, the Hon. Mrs Vernon Harcourt, provided the site and a substantial donation towards the move, and the parishioners raised the rest.

Under Church law a chancel cannot be moved, but in 1864 the rest of St Peter's was dismantled stone by stone, taken to the new site on farm carts, and reassembled. Everything went smoothly except that it was re-erected with the east end facing north. Nobody seems to know why. Perhaps it was intentional; Mrs Harcourt may have preferred it that way, or it may have fitted the site better. If it was a slip-up, it seems odd that nobody spotted it until it was too late.

Back at Church Norton the chancel was left uncared for until it was restored in 1917 and rededicated as St Wilfrid's Chapel. It has some striking modern windows. One features the Red Cross, the Green Cross of Canada, and the St John Ambulance Brigade; another shows a dozen or more animals and birds in scenes from the nature reserve in which the Chapel stands – shades of Eddi's Service. The latest addition in 1988 was the stone altar shelf on the east wall, replacing a traditional wooden altar. It all looks so attractive that perhaps one day they will want to move the rest of St Peter's back north to rejoin it – after all, it is already turned in that direction.

LEFT St Wilfrid's Chapel, once the chancel of St Peter's Church. The rest of St Peter's was moved two miles away.

4 miles N of Shoreham off the A283

It should be St Cuthman's, not St Andrew's – just ask the lady in the handcart

ST CUTHMAN WAS AN EIGHTH-century saint from Wessex who would still be patron saint of Steyning Church if it were not for the Norman monks of Fecamp. He certainly deserves to be: he built the original church, spent his life ministering to the people, and when he died and was buried there, his shrine becoming a famous place of pilgrimage, credited with powers to heal the disabled and the sick. A great stone slab in the porch of the present church is said to be associated with that period, and may even have given the village its name – the Saxon word Stenningas means 'the people of the stone'.

Throughout the existence of the original Saxon church it was dedicated to St Cuthman, with the approval of King Alfred's father, King Ethelwulf: it was on his royal estate. He was buried there too, in AD853, and the other ancient stone in the porch is said to be his coffin lid. But in the eleventh century Edward the Confessor handed over the church – and its income – to the Abbot of Fecamp, in gratitude for the hospitality he had received there during his exile, and its days as St Cuthman's were numbered.

After the Conquest the monks from Fecamp built a new and much grander church with stone shipped in from Caen, and rededicated it to St Andrew. The splendid nave with its massive circular pillars, and the great chancel arch, date back to those early days, but the church fell into decay after the

Dissolution, and in subsequent years it has been partly demolished, a new tower built where the west end of the nave used to be, the chancel rebuilt in a different style and a new sanctuary added. The monks of Fecamp might find it difficult to recognize – but it still bears the name they gave it.

Happily, St Cuthman is not forgotten. In 1983 the chapel by the chancel was dedicated to him, with a modern stained-glass window illustrating the legend of how he came to Steyning.

It is said he was travelling through Sussex, after his father died, hauling his sick mother in a home-made handcart. He pulled it by a yoke round his neck. First the yoke broke, and when he made a handle from an elder branch, that broke too. Less saintly souls might have cursed their bad luck, but Cuthman called it a sign from God that he should go no further, so he founded his church where the handcart stopped.

No doubt his mother, her bumpy journey over at last, called it a sign from God too; or was it she who frayed the yoke and broke the handle? No, let us stick to the legend ...

RIGHT The name of the village comes from the Saxon word Stenningas meaning 'the people of the stone' – and this could be the stone.

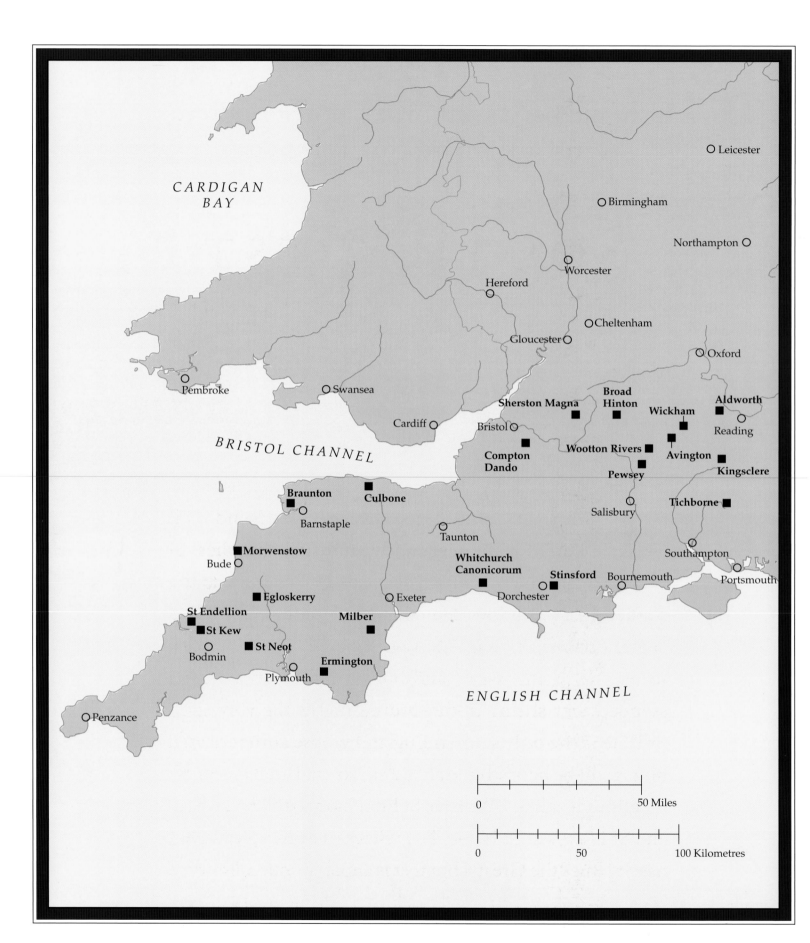

CARDIGAN BAY

Leicester

Birmingham

Northampton

Worcester

Hereford

Cheltenham

Gloucester

Oxford

Pembroke

Swansea

Sherston Magna

Broad Hinton

Wickham

Aldworth

Cardiff

Bristol

Reading

BRISTOL CHANNEL

Compton Dando

Wootton Rivers

Avington

Kingsclere

Pewsey

Braunton

Culbone

Tichborne

Barnstaple

Salisbury

Taunton

Southampton

Morwenstow

Bude

Whitchurch Canonicorum

Stinsford

Bournemouth

Portsmouth

Egloskerry

Exeter

Dorchester

St Endellion

Milber

St Kew

St Neot

Bodmin

Ermington

Plymouth

ENGLISH CHANNEL

Penzance

0   50 Miles

0   50   100 Kilometres

2
THE
SOUTH-WEST

THIS AREA HAS A MARVELLOUS ASSORTMENT OF unusual Celtic saints, who are a Godsend, as it were, for the seeker after unusual churches. St Neot, for instance, was only fifteen inches high, and a stained-glass window depicting his life has been called 'a glorious strip cartoon'. St Endellion asked for her body to be put in an ox-cart and buried wherever the oxen stopped; her shrine in the church marks the very spot. St Wite is the only saint in England whose authenticated bones still lie beneath the altar. And so on. But it can cause repetitive headings. We have St Endellion's at St Endellion, and St Neot's at St Neot. The village of St Kew, however, has St James the Great – but that is another unusual story…

3 miles W of Goring on the B4009

Slumbering giants, a yew that re-grew – and a poem to remember

MUCH OF THE SPACE IN ST MARY'S Church is taken up by the Aldworth Giants. When you sit in any of the pews you are liable to find one lying at your side, slumbering through the service. They are the fourteenth-century effigies of the de la Beche family, of whom the largest was Sir Philip, Sheriff of Berkshire and Oxfordshire, and valet to Edward II. He lies languidly on one elbow, surveying his recumbent relatives dotted among the congregation. There are nine de la Beches, and although the effigies were probably larger than life, they must have been a formidable lot.

There was a period when nobody knew which was which. It is said that when the Earl of Leicester brought Elizabeth I to see them, he took down the place-names to show her, and forgot to put them back. But last century a vicar studied some old documents and relabelled the effigies with what he thought were their names. None of them protested, and the names are there still.

Actually the locals used to have their own names for four of them: John Long, John Strong, John Ever Afraid, and John Never Afraid. Nobody seems to know why. But John Ever Afraid may have had good cause to be fearful, because his effigy was removed from its arch in an outside wall of the church. It may have happened in Cromwell's time, when all the effigies got knocked about a bit, but in spite of the dam-age they are still claimed to be unique: no other parish church, it is said, possesses anything like them.

St Mary's possesses two more claims to fame, out in the churchyard. One is an ancient yew tree, said to be a thousand years old. It was uprooted by a storm in 1976, but part still survives, and there is new growth on its propped-up branch.

The other is the memorial tablet to Laurence Binyon and his wife. His name may be unfamiliar, but the lines he wrote are heard and repeated by millions every year. They begin: 'They shall not grow old, as we that are left grow old …' As for the rest – yes, you will remember them.

RIGHT The Aldworth Giants still slumber among the congregation
OPPOSITE the yew tree still survives in the churchyard after a thousand years.

3 miles E of Hungerford, off the A4

Eleven curiously-occupied arches – and another that sags in the middle

THE DEAD-STRAIGHT 'NO THROUGH Road' which is the only route into Avington has broad, immaculately mown verges like a driveway into a private estate – and that in effect is what it is. When it peters out there is just the odd cottage and some farm buildings; a private drive continues to the Big House. There is also, just around the corner, the church of St Mark and St Luke – 'privately owned,' says the notice, 'but visitors are very welcome'.

The benefits of private ownership are very apparent. You approach it across a field, but not any old field: it is as immaculate as the grass verges. And the interior of the church seems in good shape too – except for the chancel arch. It sags in the middle in a most alarming fashion: at first sight it seems in danger of imminent collapse.

Actually it has been like that probably for centuries. It is one of those architectural quirks, like the Leaning Tower of Pisa, which can confound the experts and the laws of gravity. The dozens of carved heads which decorate it look fairly unconcerned, and they have known it longer than most.

The other feature in the church which causes brows to furrow is the font. It has eleven arches carved on it, containing strange effigies which look like deformed giants. They have very large heads and bodies, and very small legs and feet. In one arch a muscular couple stand side by side, nursing a baby; in another, a bulky figure holds a bishop's crook – and these are the only ones I could associate with a religious theme. Certainly another couple, with their arms around each other and their bodies merged, conjured up a

ABOVE AND LEFT The figures on the font still baffle the experts, and so does the sage in the chancel arch. Both have survived for many centuries.

quite different train of thought.

Even the great Pevsner seemed to give up on this font, after calling it 'exceptionally interesting'. And why eleven arches, one wonders. There are fonts with Seven Sacraments, Ten Commandments, Twelve Labours of the Month – but how many are divided into eleven? Maybe the mason just ran out of space.

The church is only used for the occasional wedding or funeral these days, and the bell no longer hangs in the gable because the woodwork isn't safe. It now stands on the floor near the font. I hope the sight of it does not give the chancel arch any ideas about giving up the struggle too – so it decides to sag a little further, and prove the experts right after all.

7 miles NW of Newbury on the B4000

The 'angels' in the roof
– with tusks, trunks and big floppy ears

THERE ARE PLENTY OF ANGELS in church roofs, but not many like the ones in the north aisle of St Swithun's. Instead of the regulation wings they have very large ears, and instead of the usual scrolls or shields they have tusks and trunks. These 'angels' are papier-mâché elephants, painted gold with stripes around their tusks, and bedecked with tasselled cloths round their necks and on their heads. It is difficult to picture a more unlikely decoration in the roof of a traditional English country church.

Were they the gift of some passing Sultan, perhaps, who thought they might cheer up the old medieval building, and the parishioners did not have the nerve to say no? Quite the contrary. They were installed by the Revd William Nicholson, a nineteenth-century incumbent of St Swithun's who decided to restore his church, as did so many wealthy Victorian parsons, but added a few touches of his own.

He went to the Paris Exhibition in search of angels for the roof, and four papier-mâché elephants took his fancy as well – so he ordered another four to make up the set. But the last part of the Sultan story is probably true: the parishioners did not have the nerve to say no …

There are other cosmopolitan features in St Swithun's, as well as an octet of French elephants. The font cover was worked in New Zealand in about the same period, and a chalice pall on show in a glass case alongside a sixteenth-century chasuble came from a church in Spain.

The most home-grown feature of the church is its tower, the oldest in Berkshire, built by the Saxons reusing Roman tiles and stonework. It is often suggested that church towers were originally built as watch towers, with little evidence to confirm it, but St Swithun's has a blocked-in doorway halfway up, which the watchman entered by ladder, then pulled it up behind him in case of attack, and there are slots for the beams which supported his warning beacon. If he had seen the approach of a herd of golden papier-mâché elephants, he might well have lit it!

BELOW One of the golden papier-mâché elephants a former rector acquired at the Paris Exhibition and put in the church roof.

5 miles NW of Launceston off the A395

A medieval effigy too big for this niche? let's chop off its feet!

THE ORIGINAL NORMAN CHURCH WAS just dedicated to St Keri or St Keria – nobody seems quite sure whether the name is male or female. It was not until 1730 that St Petroc was adopted as joint patron saint, and the church's patronal festival is celebrated on his day, June 4th – perhaps because, again, nobody is quite sure which day is St Keri's (or St Keria's).

Even the double influence of two patron saints, however, could not prevent one of the most astonishing examples in the country of heavy-handed Victorian 'restoration'. Fortunately it did not apply to the whole church, but mainly to the fifteenth-century alabaster effigy of Sir Guy de Albo Monasterio. Sir Guy, who semi-Anglicized his name to Blanchminster, was the fourth child of the Lord of Stratton, and as it turned out, the last of the line. He died in 1404, and his effigy wears a long gown, has a chain around the neck and a large purse at the waist, to indicate his generous donations to charity.

It used to lie in the north transept, but when the Victorians went into action in 1886 it was moved to its present niche below the east window. As the church guide says: 'It was probably damaged in the process, for the nose has been crudely restored.' Ah well, these things happen. But it goes on, quite laconically: 'In order to fit the effigy into an already existing recess, the feet were removed, and the rosettes from the slippers were placed upon the breast for safe keeping…'

The feet were removed! How lucky they did not leave the feet and remove the head. But at least the rosettes, removed for safe keeping, are still safe – though their incongruous position is more suited to an exotic dancer than a learned medieval knight.

The Victorians had no such problem with Penheale pew in the north transept, which had a splendid ornate canopy on Corinthian columns. They wanted to make room for the organ – so they just removed it altogether.

However, they cannot perhaps be blamed for the damage to Grace Speccott's memorial, which has lost the bottom half of its inscription. Even so, it is a pity, because the initial letters of each line of verse spelt her name. Only the first six survive, spelling GRACE S. But happily, one of them contains the other ingenious feature of the inscription: 'Go accept rest' in the opening line is an anagram of her name.

BELOW AND RIGHT Sir Guy's effigy has the decorative rosettes from his severed feet resting on his chest, and Grace Speccott's memorial tablet has the anagram 'Rest in Peace'.

7 miles N of Bude off the A39

A Highlander on guard in the churchyard, and a 'lake' rippling over the porch

THERE IS A MEMORIAL WINDOW IN St John's to its famously eccentric Victorian vicar, the Revd Robert Hawker, but it hardly seems necessary. There are many other reminders of him, in and around the church – not least, the chimneys on the vicarage, in the shape of his favourite church towers, except for the kitchen chimney, which is said to be a copy of his mother's tomb.

On the nearby clifftop is the hut which he built out of driftwood – now one of the more dilapidated properties of the National Trust. He used to sit and meditate there, dressed in a fisherman's jersey and seaboots. This was not as odd as it sounds, because he not only meditated, he kept watch for ships in trouble. Morwenstow has one of the most dangerous coastlines in England, and he helped in many rescues – where the jersey and seaboots proved eminently practical.

He also presided at many sailors' funerals, one of which was for forty men from the *Caledonia*, an Arbroath ship which was wrecked in 1843. At his suggestion, their mass grave was marked by the ship's figurehead, a sturdy Highlander wielding a sword. Mr Hawker's eccentric reputation even extended to the Highlander: it was said that anyone walking too near it at midnight would be decapitated with the sword.

In the same year as that wreck, St John's was the scene of the first harvest festival service since medieval times; the vicar revived the idea of Christian festivals of thanksgiving at harvest time, and every church in the country now has one. But St John's may not have been decorated as elaborately as some are today: during his incumbency it was often littered with driftwood and vegetation he had collected, and he disliked anyone clearing it away. But he had a great affection for his church, with its fine Norman arches and carved heads of men and animals.

He was particularly taken with the Norman zig-zag patterning over the porch. He called it 'the ripple of the lake of Gennesareth, the spirit breathing upon the waters of baptism.' Yes, he was quite a poet too …

RIGHT If you walk too close at midnight to the mass grave he is guarding, watch out for the Higlander's sword.

4 miles N of Wadebridge on the B3314

The saint gets a cow on her coat of arms – and Betjeman gets an angel in the roof

ST ENDELLION – OR ST ENDELIENTA, as they confusingly call her in St Endellion – was one of that sizeable army of high-born hermits from Wales who became Cornish saints, leaving to posterity their shrines, sometimes their holy wells – and always their legends. Endellion, it is said, subsisted on milk from her cow, until it wandered on to the local lord's land and he killed it. Retribution was swift: the lord was killed by Endellion's godfather, who happened to be King Arthur. But Endellion, being a saint, arranged for both the lord and the cow to come back to life.

She asked that after her death her body should be put on a cart drawn by two young animals – not, presumably, the long-suffering cow – and be buried wherever they stopped. The stone shrine in the church marks the very spot.

In Norman times St Endellion's was made a collegiate church, and in spite of Henry VIII and other hazards, it still holds that status. There are stalls in the chancel for the four prebendaries, or priests, who are charged with visiting the church, assisting the rector, and praying for the College.

The church has some unusual modern adornments. In contrast to the coats of arms of three ancient Cornish families on the fifteenth-century stoup by the door, there is the blue, green and yellow coat of arms of St Endellion herself, on a charter which was only granted in 1950. It features her crown of glory, the heads of the oxen which pulled

RIGHT There is a dire penalty for any clumsy bellringer in the Ringers' Rhyme: 't'will make him careful against another time'.

her cart, and the resurrected cow, looking suitably ruminative. As another contrast, among the plain wooden angels on the rafters is a brightly-painted new one, clasping a scroll in honour of Sir John Betjeman, Poet Laureate and lover of old churches, who frequently worshipped in St Endellion's until his death in 1984.

Even more colourful, but much older, is the wall-panel illustrating the Ringers' Rhyme, which includes the dire warning: 'Who weares a hat or spurr o'erturns a Bell, Or by unskilful handling spoils a peal, Shall sixpence pay for every single crime. T'will make him careful against another time.'

These days bell-ringing is augmented by St Endellion's famous music festivals, which attract distinguished performers and large audiences. But its main role, as it has been for so many centuries, is for meditation and prayer. Sir John Betjeman summed it up: 'Inside, the church gives the impression that it goes on praying night and day, whether there are people in it or not…'

4 miles N of Wadebridge off the A39

How St Docco put the 'ow' in Lanow
– and it became St Kew

THE CHURCH DEDICATED TO ST JAMES in the village of St Kew – which seems odd in itself – has had a confusing history. The church was St Kew's for over a thousand years, until well after the fifteenth century, but for nearly all that period the village was not called St Kew but Lanow. And there was actually a chapel before St Kew's church, which was named after her brother, St Docco. So St James was a very late starter indeed.

The story of the church's foundation is so wrapped up in legend it is difficult to verify, but it seems that St Docco established a monastery – a 'lan' in the language of Cornwall in those days – called Lanow. The 'ow' apparently meant Docco, though the connection is a little obscure; perhaps he was given to pained exclamations.

His sister Kewe – she used to have an 'e' – visited Lanow and impressed him with her saintly powers by making a wild boar obey her. However, her powers did not apparently extend to bears, because she offered to build a new church for him wherever a troublesome local bear could be caught and killed by the villagers. And that is why, so it is said, the church is some way from the probable site of the monastery, on a farm which is still called Lanow.

The church was rebuilt in the fifteenth century, but it was still called St Kew until some time after that. Nobody is sure why she lost out to St James, but perhaps by then biblical figures had become more fashionable than legendary local saints. There is a reminder of her in one of the chancel's stained-glass windows, a reference to the story of the troublesome bear.

However, there is another reminder of those days which is much more concrete – or rather, granite. It is a chunk of rock inscribed with the word JUSTI, meaning the grave of Justis, in Ogham lettering, a script used by fifth century Celts. Not many people can read Ogham today, but conveniently the word is written in Roman letters too; maybe not many fifth-century Celts could read Ogham either. The stone was found by a nearby stream, where the body was presumably buried, but there is no other evidence. Certainly there is no Justis.

BELOW The Ogham stone, inscribed in fifth-century Ogham script as well as Roman letters
RIGHT A Book of Hours.

6 miles W of Liskeard off the A38

Was this St Neot a Cornish Celt, or did King Alfred play a neot trick?

ST NEOT, IT IS SAID, WAS ONLY FIFTEEN inches high, but for such a tiny saint he caused quite a lot of controversy over his origins. The Saxon lobby argues that when King Alfred visited the area and was healed at a holy well, his relative Neot was with him and got the credit. Alfred dedicated the church to him, and St Neot was eventually buried by the well. It was only later that his bones were transferred to the better-known St Neots in what used to be Huntingdonshire.

However, the Celtic lobby says that in the eleventh century the village was called St Anietus, a Celtic version of Neot. The holy well was Celtic, the ancient granite cross by the church door is Celtic – one of the finest of its kind – and everything points to the saint being Celtic too. Certainly the St Neot window in the church, 'a glorious strip cartoon' as the guidebook calls it, features one or two events in his life with a distinctly Celtic flavour.

It is one of several splendid windows, many dating from the early sixteenth century, and my favourite is another 'glorious strip cartoon' featuring Noah and his Ark. The artist was a whimsical sort of chap: as a preliminary in the adjoining window, Noah is portrayed doffing his cap to God as he receives his orders to build the Ark, and the Ark itself turns out to be a three-masted ship that is more likely to have sailed to the Americas with Columbus. The barrels he loads on board indicate his liking for a glass or two, which is confirmed by the drunken celebrations in a later panel. The barrels prompt a touch of whimsy in the guidebook too; it wonders if they inspired G. K.

Chesterton's lines: 'I don't care where the water goes, If it doesn't get into the wine…'

None of the windows was apparently damaged during the Civil War, in spite of the village's strong Royalist sympathies. Like many other Cornish churches, St Neot's proudly displays a copy of Charles I's letter of thanks to his supporters in Cornwall, painted on a board, and as a further demonstration of its loyalty there is an oak apple bough on top of the tower. It is renewed every year to mark Charles's escape in the Boscobel Oak. If Cromwell's men had foreseen that, they might have smashed a few windows in retribution; maybe St Neot – Saxon or Celt – made sure they did not.

BELOW The oak-apple bough on the tower shows support for Charles I
RIGHT The local saint takes care of his flock in the stained-glass window.

7 miles S of Ilfracombe on the A361

The pigs in the roof don't fly; their story is even stranger

HIGH UP IN THE ROOF OF ST Brannock's church, above the font, is a boss which from ground level looks rather like a golden gauntlet, but the five 'fingers' are piglets and the 'palm' of the gauntlet is a sow. It illustrates the legend of St Brannock, and one chronicler boldly suggests that 'it proves the legend to be truth', but the current church guidebook is considerably more guarded: 'it perhaps illustrates the local legend …'.

Even so, it is one of those legends which points a useful moral – and it may even be true. When Brannock came here in the fifth century, a crafty local farmer, hoping to appear generous, offered a site for Brannock's church on a distant hillside. But the village knew – and Someone Up There doubtless knew – that he should have offered a more convenient field in the village, but it was producing profitable crops.

So when the church was half-built, it mysteriously fell down. When they tried to rebuild it, it fell down again. Eventually an angel appeared and told Brannock to build where a sow was suckling her litter – which happened to be in the farmer's field. The farmer took the hint, and the church stands there today …

A small wooden figure in the chancel is believed to be St Brannock, but even that is uncertain. However, there is no doubt about another of the church's treasures, a palimpsest, which is a brass that has been used twice, one on each side, perhaps as an economy measure. It is on a tombstone, so only one side is visible, but there is a copy of the reverse showing a knight's head, which is said to be the oldest brass in Devon.

The other rarity is the 'table' in the chapel used for signing the register at weddings. It is actually a sixteenth-century Portuguese chest, with a happy couple depicted on the front and the Portuguese inscription: 'In the pleasure of God he lives, and his wife, his sons and daughter.' Perhaps it was made to celebrate a successful marriage; it could well be taken as an encouragement to the newly-weds signing the register.

BELOW Not a clenched gauntlet with too many fingers, but a sow with her piglets, part of the St Brannock legend.

10 miles E of Plymouth off the A38 on B3211

The spire bowed to a beautiful bride; it should bow to the Pinwill sisters too

CROOKED SPIRES HAVE A FASCINATION for those who relish (and sometimes embellish) a good legend. Chesterfield's spire is the most famous, and Cleobury Mortimer's in Shropshire may be the runner-up, but my favourite is at Ermington – partly because it is the least known, and partly because of its legend. It is said that a bride who came to St Peter and St Paul's was so beautiful that the spire bowed to her – and for this over-familiar gesture it has been in a permanent stoop ever since. Sceptics will say, and the guidebook very fairly points out, that like other crooked spires, unseasoned timbers have just twisted unevenly over the years – but you and I know better …

The guide adds that, although many people just come to St Peter and St Paul's to see the spire, the church itself is well worth a visit – and I can gladly agree. For devotees of brasses there is the elaborate one of William Strashleigh with his wife and daughter, all kneeling devoutly with the folds of their gowns immaculately arranged around them. Those who like quirky corners will relish the arched recess which used to hold twelve candles' supplied and kept alight by the people of Kingston four miles away; until the fifteenth century Kingston had no burial ground so their dead were brought here for burial, on condition they kept replenishing the candles. And students of historical hiccups will notice that pictures of the church in the late nineteenth century show the altar still set lengthwise, east to west, in accordance with an ancient decree which was rescinded in 1634: it must have taken time for the news to filter through.

But for me the biggest attraction is the story of the three enterprising Pinwill sisters, Mary, Esther and Violet, daughters of a rector who came to Ermington in 1880. The church needed restoring, the woodwork was beyond repair, and money was short. So the sisters learned woodcarving, and in the harness-room at the vicarage they produced

the splendid pulpit, with its panels illustrating the lives of St Peter and St Paul. They made the reredos behind the main altar, another in the Lady Chapel, the font cover, and the alabaster scene of the Adoration. They were so successful they launched a thriving business and supplied over a hundred other churches with their work.

They 'signed' their pulpit at St Peter and

1/2 mile SE of Newton Abbot

Three naves round a sanctuary
– the dream that came true

IT MAY BE UNUSUAL FOR A CHURCH completed in the 1960s to be listed as a building of special architectural importance, but the Dream Church of Milber is an unusual church. It was built on the principle that three naves are better than one, an idea which came to the parson in a dream, and became a reality.

Milber itself is nearly as new as its church. It was created after the First World War to alleviate the housing shortage in nearby Newton Abbot, and it started off with three hundred people – and no church. In five years they raised enough money to buy two acres of land and erect a wooden hut as a community centre. They were guided by the Revd William Keble Martin, a man of vision – literally. It was his vision that led to the wooden hut being replaced by the Dream Church.

His dream was so vivid that he was able to draw a sketch plan after breakfast of what he had seen. It turned out to be a church with no chancel but three naves radiating from the sanctuary. The vestries and the Lady Chapel were at matching angles to the two outside naves, so the ground plan looked like a rectangular card table with four cards at an angle in each corner. At that stage he had not worked out where the pulpit would go, but the font was tucked in the V-shaped gap between two of the naves.

By a happy coincidence – and the story of St Luke's is full of happy coincidences – Keble Martin's brother was a qualified architect, and he sent him his sketch plan. Instead of falling about when he saw it, as many 1930s architects might have done, Arthur Keble Martin became as enthusiastic as his brother. In fact, as he developed the design on the drawing-board he may have shared the vision as well, because he said the design seemed to dictate itself.

Strangest of all, when the plans were completed it was found that, entirely by happy coincidence, the church was exactly a thousand inches long – 83 feet four inches – a thousand inches broad and a thousand inches high. It did not take long for someone to recall the line about the Temple in Revelation – 'The length and the breadth and the height of it are equal' – and any final doubts about the Dream Church were dispelled.

It took thirty years, interrupted by the war, but St Luke's was completed in 1963. It is a church not only of special architectural importance, one might think, but of special hypernatural importance as well.

LEFT 'The length and breadth and the height of it are equal': the Dream Church and the Temple in Relevation.

3 miles NE of Dorchester off the A35

It was Thomas Hardy's church, but Arthur Shirley was there too

STINSFORD WAS THOMAS HARDY'S village, and St Michael's was Thomas Hardy's church, immortalized in his writings and full of memories of him. One of its showpieces is the diagram he drew of the musicians' gallery, showing where members of his family used to play in the church's string choir. He wrote a memorial inscription in Latin – not just to frustrate non-scholars, but because 'the English lan-guage is liable to undergo great alterations in the future, whereas Latin will remain unchanged'. He was right, of course, but fortunately most memorial writers these days decide to chance it.

Hardy was christened at St Michael's, became a Sunday School teacher, attended regularly, and eventually left his heart there – literally. It is buried in the churchyard; the rest of him is in Westminster Abbey. Just along the church path is the grave of his great admirer, the poet Cecil Day Lewis, buried there at his own request.

In his later years, as a qualified architect, Hardy took an active interest in the church's maintenance, and offered a lot of advice on

BELOW Here lies the heart of Thomas Hardy, a rather long grave considering that the rest of him is in Westminster Abbey.

the church bells, which was mostly taken, and on repairing the battered old oak pews, which was not. It was his idea to restore the Norman font, which was rescued from a pile of rubbish in seven pieces – but it took ten years for the idea to catch on.

All this attention from such a distinguished parishioner could have been a bit wearing for an incumbent, but one rector made a rather greater impact on the interior appearance of the church than Hardy himself – and incurred the wrath of the Hardy family in the process. The Revd Arthur Shirley came to St Michael's in 1837, three years before Hardy was born, and stayed for over fifty years. In spite of the Hardys he disbanded the string choir and substituted a barrel organ instead. The musicians' gallery went, so did the box pews and the pews in the chancel. St Michael's never looked quite the same again.

But Thomas Hardy got his own back, in his own way. He created a fictional vicar in 'Under the Greenwood Tree' who made much the same changes as Arthur Shirley, but for distinctly unworthy motives – and the fictional string choir, unlike the Hardy family, won in the end. As one biographer commented: 'He distorted ecclesiastical facts for literary benefit'.

And he might have added: 'Nothing changes …'

LEFT When the Norman font was rescued from a pile of rubbish it was in seven pieces. Thomas Hardy suggested restoring it, but it took ten years.

5 miles E of Lyme Regis off the A35

Candida may sound grander, but wite must be right

THERE HAS BEEN AS MUCH DEBATE over the name of the church's patronal saint as the identity of the saint herself. Originally St Candida was St Wite, but during the Middle Ages they switched to the Latinized version. The guidebook hedges its bets and calls it 'The Church of St Candida (St Wite) …' but the saint's tomb is still known as St Wite's. Certainly if she was a Saxon saint, why call her by a Latin name?

Some say they are not sure if she was, even though it was believed for centuries that she was a Saxon anchorite who fell foul of a band of marauding Danes and became a Virgin Martyr. King Alfred was so upset he founded a church for her shrine, so the story goes, and William the Conqueror was also impressed by her story – or perhaps the prosperity of the village as a result of it – and

appointed his personal chaplain Guntard to the benefice. Guntard dismantled the Saxon church and started on a new one, which was completed at the end of the twelfth century. It has been added to since, but still possesses some of the finest Early English work in Dorset, and St Wite's present tomb also dates from that period.

In recent times, however, new theories about the saint have been suggested. It was said she was a Breton princess who was brought to England by pirates, but she escaped and walked home – across the waters of the English Channel. Her relics were brought back years later by Breton refugees. A more bizarre version was that Wite was actually a Wessex monk called Witta, but this theory rather collapsed when the tomb cracked open during structural work on the masonry, and in the stone cof-

fin was a leaden one containing the bones of a woman of the Saxon period, aged about forty. The lead coffin was inscribed: 'Here rest the remains of St Wite.. The case for St Wite rests.

St Candida-née-Wite's can therefore claim to be the only parish church in the country containing the authenticated relics of its patron saint. They are in the upper part of the shrine, and below are three oval holes in the stonework through which pilgrims put their diseased limbs to be healed by the aura of St Wite's remains. It happens less frequently now, but offerings and petitions are still put inside the holes, in honour of the Danes' victims of so many centuries ago. King Alfred would be delighted.

BELOW St Wite's tomb has holes for diseased limbs. Stomach aches could be a problem.

9 miles NW of Basingstoke on the A339

Henry IV met his bride here – and King John met a bed-bug

AS YOU WOULD ASSUME FROM ITS NAME, Kingsclere has royal connections, dating back to King Alfred. It was part of the Royal estate, and the church was the estate's main place of worship, but most of the visiting royals were more interested in hunting than worshipping. St Mary's does have the carved heads of Henry IV and his second wife Queen Joan in the nave, but it is not suggested that they ever visited the church. It just so happened that the king had to wait in the vicinity for the delayed arrival of his bride from Brittany, to escort her to their nuptials – not in St Mary's, but in Winchester Cathedral.

The church has another Royal memento, but the occasion it commemorates is not so felicitous. King John found himself fog-bound in Kingsclere after a hunting-expedition, and stayed at a local inn, where he had an unfortunate encounter with a bed-bug. Much irritated – in every sense – he ordered that a large replica of a bed-bug should be displayed on the church tower as a dreadful warning to other travellers.

The church made the best of things and utilized the bug as a weathervane – and the tower has been 'bugged' ever since. The present one, erected in 1751, is a rather elegant creature with delicate little crosses for legs. It has become quite a tourist attraction, which is exactly the opposite of what King John had in mind!

The inn he stayed at – which by rights should have displayed the bed-bug, not the church – was happily not the Golden Falcon, Kingsclere's best-known inn until it became a private house. The Fawconers, whose arms incorporated three falcons,

were a leading local family, and they gave the church most of its valuable plate. These days it is on display in Winchester Cathedral Treasury, but there is no shifting a gift from another family, the Porters: they gave the stained-glass windows in the north transept. John Porter owned the local racing stables and among the traditional biblical scenes, they have included his horse Ormonde, said

by racing buffs to be one of the finest race-horses of the English turf.

So far as Kingsclere's reputation is concerned, Ormonde must make up for that bed-bug.

BELOW King John intended the bed-bug on the church tower to deter visitors; actually it attracts them.

5 miles E of Winchester off the A31

An RC chapel in an Anglican church – another Tichborne claim to fame

IT IS RARE FOR A TINY VILLAGE TO BECOME widely known for two quite different reasons, but the Tichborne Dole and the Tichborne Claimant have both earned their own places in the history books. The Dole was instituted after the dying wife of a thirteenth-century squire managed to crawl round a 23-acre field so he would bequeath the crops from it to a charity for the poor, and the Claimant appeared during the last century after the squire's heir was feared lost at sea – but turned out to be a butcher's son from Wapping.

Neither story is connected directly with St Andrew's, but the church contains many monuments to the Tichborne family – and it has its own claim to fame, as perhaps the only Anglican country church in England in which the north aisle continued to be used as a Roman Catholic chapel after the Reformation.

The Tichbornes became lords of the manor about 1135, not long after the earli-

BELOW Sir Richard Tichborne's infant son was drowned as prophesied, in spite of precautions.

est part of the church was built; the chancel dates from the eleventh century. Throughout the Reformation and the difficult years that followed they remained steadfast Roman Catholics. They suffered much persecution, but Sir Benjamin Tichborne survived as High Sheriff of Hampshire, and when James I came to the throne in 1603 he rode to Winchester and declared his allegiance to the new king. They became good friends, and presumably it was because of this that the north aisle of St Andrew's was allowed to continue in use as a Catholic chapel for the Tichbornes.

It contains a fine alabaster monument to Sir Benjamin, dated 1621. He is depicted lying beside his wife Amphillis, with their seven children kneeling below them. The box pews from the same period have been preserved, but unfortunately a medieval wall-painting of St Christopher has been lost. The guidebook observes, rather casually, that it is 'perhaps obscured beneath a coat of whitewash…'

The other Tichborne monuments include one to Sir Richard Tichborne's infant son, victim of another bizarre incident in the family's eventful history. An unfriendly gypsy laid a curse on the baby boy, saying he would die by drowning on a particular day. Sir Richard had his son taken to high ground on that day, well away from any river, but the baby fell out of its carriage and drowned in a cart-rut full of water.

LEFT Sir Benjamin Tichborne lies in state beside his wife Amphillis, with his seven children kneeling beneath them.

5 miles W of Porlock off the A39

It may be tiny but it has seen lepers, a murder, and a visit from St Michael

ST BEUNO'S IS SO TINY AND ISOLATED that one could almost believe its main purpose it to provide a tourist attraction and to qualify for the *Guinness Book of Records* – and indeed it has achieved both. But this is a living church, in regular use, and although the number of names in the visitors' book per week is probably greater than can be accommodated in its pews, and there are only thirty-odd people in Culbone anyway, it only qualified as a record-holder because it is the smallest complete medieval church 'still in use'.

Even so, it is difficult to understand why it was built in such an inaccessible place. There is no road to it, just a half-mile rocky track down the combe or a footpath along the coast from Porlock Weir. There used to be cottages nearby, but at one stage in the sixteenth century the locals were outnumbered by fifty lepers, men, women and children, who were deposited in the woods to fend for themselves. They were not allowed to mix with the villagers, but they could watch services in St Beuno's through the leper squint which can still be seen in the north wall. They stayed in the combe until

BELOW The spirelet on the tiny church was a present, so it is said, from St Michael.

they died; one arrived as a baby and was there for nearly eighty years.,

This deceptively idyllic setting has seen not only a leper colony but a medieval penal settlement and an eighteenth-century camp for prisoners-of-war; its isolation made it ideal for all these purposes. St Beuno's has even had one of its priests convicted of murder. In 1280, according to the local Assize Rolls, the chaplain of Culbone, called Thomas, 'struck Albert of Ash on the head with a hatchet, and so killed him'. Life in Culbone, it seems, was never dull.

There is even a dramatic story attached to St Beuno's itself. There were no doubt some exciting moments during its construction, as the stones and timbers were manoeuvred down the steep hillside, but the arrival of its little spirelet, according to legend, was even more spectacular. Apparently it was brought there by St Michael, no less. It originally formed the top of the spire on Porlock church, but the locals had done something naughty, and the Archangel shortened their spire as a punishment.

He must have sliced it off at just the right height: the spirelet fits the roof of St Beuno's perfectly.

LEFT In spite of its inaccessibility, St Beuno's attracts thousands of tourists every year. Cynics suggest that is why it was built there – but the church is alive and in regular use.

8 miles W of Bath off the A39

Their Roman altar is back in Bath and the Saxon cross has vanished, but the Dando bird flies on

ST MARY'S HAS NOT HAD A LOT OF LUCK with its ancient relics. An antiquarian who visited Compton Dando in 1826 came across two of them in the stable-yard at the vicarage. One was a Saxon stone carved with runic scrolls – 'and there is little doubt,' he wrote, 'it formed part of a highly ornamental cross'; it has now vanished without trace. The other was an early Norman font, being used as a water-trough, and he noted with disgust: 'An ugly painted basin stands substitute in one of the pews'. The church does have a proper font again, but no one can tell if it was the one in the stableyard.

The antiquarian did however spot a third relic, a cornerstone from a Roman altar built into a buttress of the church, and I saw it there myself in 1993. The figures on it were Hercules and Apollo, and St Mary's liked to claim it had the two oldest supporters of any church in the country. It presumably found its way there from Bath – no one knows how or why – and Bath had been trying for nearly thirty years to get it back – without success.

'The majority opinion seems to come down firmly on the side of 'what we have, we hold', said the church booklet at the time. 'There can never be actual proof that the stone was removed from Bath, but even assuming it was, what a vast upheaval of antiquities there would be if it was decided that all should be returned to their original sites!'

There was another factor however: the elements were wearing away the ancient stone. It was glassed in for a time, but that made it worse. In 1996 the Church Council admitted defeat and allowed it to be removed and put on display in Bath Museum.

However, there is still quite a lot to see at St Mary's, apart from a buttress with a hole in it. One window, for instance, has stained-glass shields which are said to have come from City of London churches after the Great Fire. There is the curious creature on the eighteenth-century weathervane, which an archdeacon christened the Dando Bird – Dando, incidentally, has nothing to do with dandies but derives from the local de Alno family. And the churchyard has a row of 250-year-old lime trees and some other fine old trees – unfortunately one of them blew down in 1899 on top of the ancient lychgate and completely destroyed it. So, alas, St Mary's has not had much luck with lychgates either. But as the current guidebook says gamely, from the bridge over the River Chew the medieval tower and the fine cedar that flanks it make a proud silhouette against the setting sun – 'and long may they stand'. The new lychgate probably hopes so too.

BELOW The church has lost many of its treasures, but is does have a real font again.

6 miles S of Swindon off the A4361

A tower which 'stood on three legs', and a monument – look, no hands …

ST PETER'S WAS REBUILT IN 1634, AND not much remains of its earliest days, but the fifteenth-century tower still survives – even though for a time it had to balance on three legs.

A dramatic emergency repair job was carried out in 1928, because one of the piers supporting the tower arch was bulging inwards, nearly a foot off the perpendicular. The wall was shored up while the base was taken away and new foundations were sunk.

During this tricky operation a gale blew up which could have caused a disaster, but 'the tower on three legs', as the church guide describes it, stood firm.

As well as the tower, one or two monuments in St Peter's date back to the 1400s, notably those of the local landowners until the Civil War, the Wroughtons. The tomb of Sir Thomas Wroughton, his wife Anne and their eight children, causes great debate, because Sir Thomas's effigy has no hands,

and nor have any of the children. On the other hand (one might say), his wife has both of hers, and they hold a Bible.

Sir Thomas combined the duties of Sheriff of Wiltshire with poaching the king's deer, and as the guide delicately puts it: 'He may have been someone who was not always ready to conform'. It does not seem greatly out of character, therefore, that when he came home from a hunting trip and found his wife reading a Bible instead of preparing his supper, he threw the Bible in the fire. That at least is the legend; there are various versions of what happened next.

Some say his hands withered away as a punishment, and the blight fell on his children as well. Others claim he repented, and lost his hands when he plunged them in the fire to retrieve the Bible. The more cynical theory is that the hands were knocked off by Cromwell's troopers, who knocked off the children's as well – and indeed, Broad Hinton was a very Royalist village. But why did Anne's hands survive – and why was there no other damage?

There is no debate about Colonel Francis Glanville's monument – but only just. He fought for Charles I and died in the siege of Bridgwater, aged twenty-eight. The Latin inscription boldly announces: 'A greater hero England never saw.' Supporters of Henry V, Wellington, Nelson and many others will be muttering 'Francis who?', but they can subside. The second line wisely adds the qualification: 'Ah, happy did she oft produce his equal …'

LEFT *The Wroughton memorial is imposing – but a little short on hands.*

6 miles S of Marlborough on the A345

Rafters from a priory, rails from a warship, and wing feathers from - whom?

S T JOHN'S IS ONE OF THOSE CHURCHES where apparently unexciting items can have a most unusual history. The rafters over the organ chamber, for instance, came from the refectory of Ivychurch Priory. It was founded by Henry II, dissolved by Henry VIII, and fell into decay until it was demolished in 1888. It so happened that St John's was being restored at the time, the Earl of Radnor owned the timber – and his son, Canon Bouverie, was the rector.

Canon Bouverie, in fact, paid the major cost of the restoration, and used his skill as a woodcarver to refurbish the church. During his thirty years' ministry he carved the altar and reredos and the pieta in the chancel, a bas relief of the Virgin Mary grieving over the dead Christ. Even after he retired in 1910 he kept on carving. He made the font cover as a memorial to the fallen in the 1914–18 War, and carved their names in stone on the south wall.

The alms box and altar rails, however, were not his work: they come under Items with Odd Histories. The lock of the alms box came from the convict settlement at Port Arthur in Tasmania, and the mahogany altar rails from a Spanish warship, the *San Joseph*, captured by Nelson off Cape St Vincent in 1797. No explanation is given about their presence in St John's; is it possible that a Pewsey burglar was sent to the penal colony and donated the lock as a reminder of his talents? And

was one of the sailors who boarded the *San Joseph* a Pewsey carpenter with a hacksaw and a big sack?

I am inclined to believe almost anything in connection with St John's, after hearing what was found in a recess in one of the pillars during that restoration work in 1888. They may have looked very like goosefeathers, but in Pewsey the story is they came from the wings of the Archangel Gabriel. Apparently Zacharias, John the

Baptist's father, clutched at him after receiving the news of his son's forthcoming birth, and was left with a handful of feathers. And sure enough, a Crusader from Pewsey acquired them in the Holy Land and brought them home. It was all taken seriously enough for the recess to be glassed over, and there are still a few feathers inside. Maybe my ideas about the convict and the sailor-carpenter are not so far-fetched after all …

RIGHT Sceptics suggest there are just goose feathers in there; only Gabriel can prove they are his.

5 miles SW of Malmesbury on the B4040

A tale of two heroes: one is in the churchyard, is that the other on the porch?

THE CHURCH OF THE HOLY CROSS has examples of almost every style of church architecture from its Norman arcade in the nave to its rebuilt Georgian tower. With a bit of imagination one could add the odd example of Saxon work in the south wall; rather more imagination is needed to solve some of the little conundrums which the builders left behind.

For instance, there are archaeological puzzles like the reason for the lonely Norman arch on the south side of the nave. Was it part of a south transept, or did it belong to an early chancel, and got moved? But perhaps more interesting to the layman are questions like the identity of the little carved heads on some of the pillars.

The church guide, very precise on most features of Holy Cross, is delightfully vague about these heads. 'A King, possibly Henry III' … 'a man, possibly Simon de Montfort' … 'A woman wearing a wimple, possibly Ela, Countess of Salisbury' … and so on. In view of all this cheerful guesswork, I am not too disheartened by the scepticism in the guide about the stone effigy high up on the outside of the porch.

I have always understood this to be John Rattlebone, the local hero who defeated King Canute's army at the Battle of Sherston in 1016. Actually, Rattlebone was quite a mercenary hero, almost to the point of blackmail, judging by a local rhyme that has come down through the centuries:

'Fight well, Rattlebone, thou shall have Sherston.'

'What shall I with Sherston do, without I have all belongs thereto?'

'Thou shalt have Wyck and Willesly, Easton Towne and Pinkeney … '

Perhaps because of this rather grasping attitude, the guide does not like the idea of having Rattlebone on the porch. It says that, in spite of local tradition, the figure is almost certainly a priest in vestments: 'a similarity to that of Archbishop Stigand in the Bayeux Tapestry has been noted'. However, it does not explain what the connection could be between the Archbishop and Sherston Magna – though the use of some more imagination could always produce a good story. But personally, I would sooner rattle the bones for Rattlebone.

Happily there is no argument about Sherston's other hero, buried in the churchyard. Twenty-one-year-old Private George Strong fought in the Crimea, and also displayed great bravery. He did not get Sherston, Wyck and Willesly, Easton Towne and Pinkeney; instead he was one of the first recipients of the Victoria Cross.

LEFT AND BELOW There are doubts about John Rattlebone, but none about Sherston Magna's other hero, George Strong.

PRIVATE
GEORGE STRONG V.C.
COLDSTREAM GUARDS
APRIL 1833 - 25. AUGUST 1888

SEVASTOPOL SEPTEMBER 1855

5 miles S of Marlborough off the A346

The lightest ring of bells in Wiltshire – and the cheapest church clock in the country?

WOOTTON RIVERS IS ONE OF those discreet little villages which rarely stars in the travel books, and St Andrew's rarely appears in architectural works of reference. But the little church has two notable features, both housed in its little wooden turret: its set of bells, and its clock.

The five bells are the lightest ring in Wiltshire. The heaviest is only three-and-a-half hundredweight, quite a minnow as church bells go. They were cast as a complete set two hundred years ago, but for the last fifty of those years they have not been able to ring, because of the condition of the bell-frame and the tower. As a project for the Millennium, the parish hopes to raise

ABOVE The southern face of the church clock, whose message is more to do with eternity than with time.

£40,000 to get them ringing again.

Happily the clock is in better shape, although it needs some attention. But considering its origins it is remarkable that it still functions at all. It must surely claim the record as the cheapest church clock in the country – made entirely from scrap!

It was the work of a self-taught clock repairer, John Kingstone Spratt, universally known as Jack. Whatever Jack Spratt's views were on the nutritional value of fat, he certainly liked clocks, and when the village decided to install one to mark George V's coronation, but found the estimates too high, he offered to make it for them for nothing, so long as they could provide 'a few hundredweight of steel, iron, brass and lead'.

So Wootton Rivers produced its old farm implements and domestic scrap, from threshing-wheels and chaff-cutters to old bedsteads and prams. Jack cut wood patterns for castings to be made at a Pewsey foundry, and some of the parts were beaten out by the village blacksmith. He assembled the clock, fitted the striking mechanism which he designed himself, and provided three faces to go on three sides of the turret. It was all finished, appropriately, on time, and the clock was dedicated on Coronation Day, 1911. Jack has long since gone – or he might have been able to help with that bell-frame – but his grandson still winds the clock by hand every week.

The final touch of this ingenious clock-maker was to substitute letters for figures on the southern face of St Andrew's unique clock. They spell, again, very appropriately: 'GLORY BE TO GOD'.

BELOW The church clock was made entirely from scrap in 1911 by an amateur clockmaker; his grandson still winds it up.

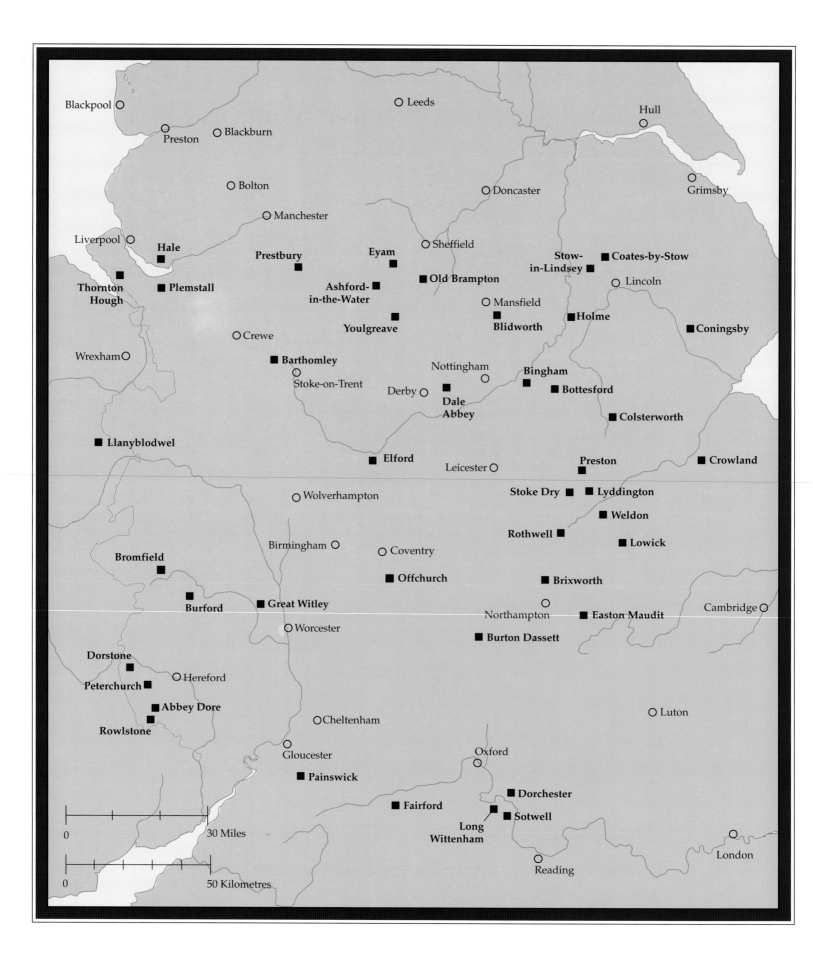

Blackpool ○

○ Leeds

Hull ○

Preston ○

○ Blackburn

○ Bolton

○ Doncaster

Grimsby ○

○ Manchester

Liverpool ○

Hale ■

○ Sheffield

Prestbury ■

Eyam ■

Stow-in-Lindsey ■

Coates-by-Stow ■

Thornton Hough ■

Plemstall ■

Ashford-in-the-Water ■

Old Brampton ■

Lincoln ○

○ Mansfield

Holme ■

Coningsby ■

○ Crewe

Youlgreave ■

Blidworth ■

Wrexham ○

Barthomley ■

Nottingham ○

Bingham ■

Stoke-on-Trent ○

Derby ○

Dale Abbey ■

Bottesford ■

Colsterworth ■

Llanyblodwel ■

Elford ■

Leicester ○

Preston ■

Crowland ■

○ Wolverhampton

Stoke Dry ■ **Lyddington** ■

Weldon ■

Rothwell ■

Lowick ■

Bromfield ■

Birmingham ○

○ Coventry

Offchurch ■

Brixworth ■

Burford ■

Great Witley ■

○ Northampton

Easton Maudit ■

Cambridge ○

○ Worcester

Burton Dassett ■

Dorstone ■

○ Hereford

Peterchurch ■

Abbey Dore ■

Luton ○

Rowlstone ■

○ Cheltenham

○ Gloucester

Oxford ○

Painswick ■

Fairford ■

Dorchester ■

Long Wittenham ■

Sotwell ■

Reading ○

London ○

0 ————————— 30 Miles

0 ————————— 50 Kilometres

3

CENTRAL ENGLAND

THIS AREA NOT ONLY HAS MANY MEMORABLE churches, it has many memorable church guidebooks. Inevitably there are exceptions. I have sifted through many close-printed pages of architectural and archaeological data in search of an occasional nugget. But places like Dale Abbey in Derbyshire and Lastingham in Yorkshire, Fairford in Gloucestershire and Plemstall in Cheshire, offer an attractive cover, lots of illustrations, and an understandable text in legible print. I am grateful to all compilers of church guides, who are often anony mous and nearly always voluntary. In particular my thanks to those who not only provide technical information for the experts, but entertaining background stories and even lighthearted trivia for the likes of me.

5 miles E of Crewe off the B5077

Almost a comedy of errors
– except for the slaughter in the tower

ST BERTOLINE'S IS A SPLENDID-LOOKING church with some splendid monuments and furnishings, but it also has a few intriguing little errors to delight the more observant. You might assume that the first error is its name: in a village called Barthomley it sounds as if the church should be St Bartholemew's. But the saint really was called Bertoline, an eighth-century local who performed a miracle where the church now stands – nobody knows what it was – and it is the village's name which has been corrupted.

The actual errors are less obvious, like the stained-glass window in the south aisle depicting three apostles, Peter, John and James the Great. But James is shown holding a fuller's club, the emblem of James the Less, a different saint altogether. 'Obviously the artist has not made a sufficiently careful study of his Bible' says the guide-book, rather primly.

The little slip-up on the carved panels of the sixteenth-century altar is easier to spot. They depict the Nativity and the Flight into Egypt, and the three Wise Men around the manger are wearing what look like jackets, trousers and top-hats. It is actually Elizabethan dress, the normal wear when the panels were carved, and no odder than, say, the Roman-era saints in medieval armour who crop up on medieval rood screens. But the guidebook cannot resist a gentle dig. 'We do not know whether the craftsman was conscious of this anachronism …'

Churchwardens are normally allocated their own pews, but St Bertoline's has one reserved for the bell-ringers. Their pew in the north aisle is carved with six bells – which is another little inaccuracy, because these days there are eight, but this time no one can blame the carver – the extra two were added much later, in 1908.

However, the greatest error in St Bertoline's occurred much earlier, in 1643, when twelve villagers were slaughtered by Royalist troops in the church tower. A contemporary account puts the blame on a Major Connaught, who smoked them down from the tower and had them stripped and killed, while he personally cut the throat of the rector's son, John Fowler. But in fact the initial error was Fowler's, and the guidebook, so critical of smaller errors, does not baulk at pointing out this one too. 'In fairness it must be said that the villagers were armed, and John Fowler foolishly fired on the soldiers from the tower, killing one of their number and provoking revenge.'

BELOW Top-hatted Wise Men
RIGHT The wrong St James with the Apostles.

5 miles W of Widnes off the A561

A church hit by fire, a parish hit by VAT but nothing could ever hit 'the child of Hale'

IT IS NOT UNUSUAL FOR A COUNTRY church to have a symbolic flight of angels in the roof, but at St Mary's it might be more appropriate to have the odd phoenix up there instead, because this is a new church which has risen from the ashes of the old. In 1977 only the four-teenth-century tower and the ruined walls of the nave survived a disastrous fire – and those ruined walls left the parish in the worst of all possible financial worlds.

There was enough of them left for the work to be considered a renovation, not a new building, so it incurred VAT. But there was not enough of them left to qual-ify for a grant for restoring an historic building. It meant that the parish, already trying to make up a substantial shortfall in the insurance cover, was also faced with an extra VAT bill of £34,000. Local MPs fought on their behalf without success. Twenty years later the battle against VAT on church restoration still goes on in Parliament – and in Hale they are still pay-ing the bill.

Nevertheless, in three years St Mary's was re-dedicated, with those unhelpful walls now spanned by a new roof of chest-nut, the work of one master carpenter. Nearly all the furnishings were lost, but nineteenth-century pews were acquired from a church near Wigan due for demo-lition, a church at Stoke-on-Trent gave the wooden eagle lectern, and most striking of all, the sixteenth-century oak pulpit came

RIGHT A curious figure at Hale, carved from the trunk of a tree and covered in marine symbols ...

from York Minster. Hale's original sandstone font, replaced by the Victorians and demoted to being a garden ornament, came in from the cold and resumed its proper role. No trace remained of the six hatchments of the Ireland Blackburne family, the local squires for many centuries, but reproductions were made from photographs taken before the fire.

While all of this was happening above him, the Childe of Hale continued to slumber in the churchyard, underneath his outsize gravestone. It records that he was born in 1578 and died in 1623 – and also, unusually for a gravestone, his height. The 'childe' was in fact nine feet three inches tall, with limbs to match: his hands, for instance, were 8 ½ inches across and 17 inches from wrist to fingertips. We know these statistics so precisely because in the eighteenth century someone suggested his size had been exaggerated, and the poor chap's body was dug up for the measurements to be checked. It seems rather a drastic way to settle an argument.

Not surprisingly, Middleton was a formidable fighter, and Sir Gilbert Ireland took him to London to challenge the King's Champion. He beat him easily and the King gave him £20, a small fortune. It might have come in handy towards that VAT.

LEFT The wording on John Middelton's gravestone is rather tricky to follow, but the height of the 'Childe' is quite clear.

3 miles NE of Chester off the A56

'His dedicated hand worked so long to the glory of the master carpenter …'

IN ST PETER'S THERE IS A WOODEN carving of a Saxon saint, in traditional gown and carrying a staff and a Bible, but with a remarkably youthful, almost twentieth-century face. The statue brings together the two men who played significant roles in the church's history, eleven centuries apart: St Plegmund, who founded it, and the Revd Joseph Hooker Toogood, who was its rector for thirty-seven years.

Plegmund later became adviser to King Alfred, who made him Archbishop of Canterbury, and he is buried in Canterbury Cathedral. But Plemstall still has St Plegmund's Well, where he baptized his converts, and its water was still used for baptisms in the church font until the level got too low.

His statue is a comparatively minor example of Hooker Toogood's work, after he came to Plemstall in 1907. There is hardly a wooden furnishing in St Peter's which he did not either restore or make himself. They range from the massive rood beam with its eighteen figures surmounted by the Crucifixion, to the offertory box by the main door. The elaborate reredos and altar, the pews, the lectern, the upper half of the chapel screen, the decorations and figures on the war memorial, the baptistry screen, the font cover – he did the lot. The only major item he did not actually work on was the eighteenth-century three-decker pulpit; instead he shifted it into the north aisle to give him more room to embellish the nave.

There are other items of interest in and around the church, of course, not least the rather creepy Hurleston tomb in the churchyard, with two skeletons sprawled on the sides. John Hurlestone was a master mariner who sailed with Drake, and was commemorated much more attractively on the postage stamps issued in 1988 to mark the four hundredth anniversary of the Armada.

But at St Peter's it is difficult to avoid or ignore the prolific handiwork of Joseph Hooker Toogood. One of his admirers wrote: 'He spent thirty-seven years preaching on the seventh day and teaching on the other six – a quiet country parson whose dedicated hand worked so long to the glory of the Master Carpenter …'

BELOW An example of the prolific work of the Revd Joseph Hooker Toogood.

3 miles N of Macclesfield off the A523

The Norman chapel was only thirty years old, but they wanted to start afresh

WHEN ST PETER'S WAS BUILT IN 1220 there was already a Norman chapel on the site, built less than thirty years before, but it was decided to ignore it and start from scratch. Both buildings have survived ever since, as an oratory and a parish church, a remarkable medieval combination rarely found in a country churchyard.

The chapel can be accurately dated, it is thought, because one of the seven figures in niches above the splendid Norman arched doorway depicts Richard I, who only reigned from 1190 to 1199. The little building was allowed to fall into ruin until Sir William Meredith restored it in 1747, and in return the Merediths were allowed to use it as their family mausoleum. There are still occasional services in it, and in 1977 new windows were dedicated in memory of the vicar's wife. Six of them illustrate a poem on an old grandfather clock in Chester Cathedral:

When as a child I laughed and wept,
   time crept.
When as a youth I dreamed and talked,
   time walked.
When I became a full-grown man,
   time ran,
And later, as I older grew,
   time flew.
Soon I shall find, while travelling on,
   time gone;
Will Christ have saved my soul by then?
   Amen.

Meanwhile in St Peter's, evidence was found of the much earlier Christian use of this site. During repairs to the chancel in 1841, pieces of ornamented sandstone were found embedded in the masonry. They fitted together to form part of a Saxon cross, probably eighth-century, which no doubt marked the arrival of Christianity in this area. It is now in a glass case in the churchyard.

A few years later the original pulpit was discovered, though it had not been hidden quite so long. It had been made in 1607 from local oak trees, but a century later it was clad in mahogany and incorporated with a clerk's desk and prayer desk to form a 'three-decker'. Workmen came across it during repairs in 1858, and it was restored to its original form.

St Peter's is rich in early memorials and tablets, and there are early eighteenth-century wall-paintings of the apostles and the twelve tribes of Israel. These were the work of an itinerant artist who had another commission in Prestbury, to paint a sign for the local inn, the Saracen's Head. Unfortunately he assumed Saracens were black, and painted the sign accordingly – so the pub's name was changed for a while to the Black Boy.

Happily he did not make a similar slip-up with the apostles.

LEFT The Norman chapel that has survived in the churchyard alongside the medieval church.

2 miles NW of Bakewell off the A6

They sold the font and moved the tympanum but no one touches the virgins' crants

SOME OF THE ANCIENT FEATURES OF Holy Trinity have had quite eventful careers since they were first installed in the church, many centuries ago. The font, for instance, octagonal, chalice-shaped, and dating back to the turn of the fifteenth century, was actually sold by the church-wardens a couple of centuries ago, and was used as a rather up-market garden ornament in a local garden. When it was eventually returned to the church – did the church-wardens buy it back, one wonders – not surprisingly the lower part of the shaft was damaged, and has been replaced. But the stone dragon embedded in it still survives, with its head and tail sticking out on each side.

Similarly, the Norman tympanum from above the main door was discovered, in the last century, embedded in the south wall of the church. It could hardly have been sold by the churchwardens to a local stonemason when he was carrying out repairs; perhaps they just disliked the look of it, since it features wild boars and other unfriendly creatures. It has now been put back over the door.

Holy Trinity's most famous relics have also 'gone walkabout' over the years. There used to be seven maidens' garlands, or virgins' crants, hanging in the church. By 1900 only five survived, and one of them fell down in the 1930s and disappeared, but the remaining four are now safely protected inside perspex covers.

The garlands traditionally consisted of a rush or wooden frame decorated with white paper rosettes. Sometimes there was a white glove too – symbolic of the gauntlet thrown down by the maiden's champion if anyone cast aspersions on her virginity. They were carried before the coffin when an unmarried virgin died – not only in Ashford, but in villages as far afield as Hampshire and Suffolk. After the funeral they were sometimes hung above the family's pew, as a rather depressing reminder of their loss. The oldest in Holy Trinity is thought to date from 1747; the most recent was carried at Elizabeth Blackwell's funeral in 1801, after she drowned in the River Wye.

Holy Trinity's other treasure is an inlaid marble table, which won a medal in 1882. The Ashford Marble industry was founded by Henry Watson in 1748, but by this century the foreign competition was too much. His works are now a depot for the local Water Board, and Henry himself is buried in the churchyard – with a memorial of his own Ashford Marble.

BELOW One of the virgin's crants, now protected inside a perspex cover.

3 miles SW of Ilkestone off the A6096

The semi-detached 'cathedral' that was once a little peculiar

DALE ABBEY WAS ONE OF THE casualties of Henry VIII's Reformation, but its infirmary and chapel, in a separate building, survived. They adjoined each other, linked by two doors, so patients could be taken through for services. When the abbey was dissolved the chapel continued to function as All Saints' and the infirmary became a private house. As a result All Saints' is that great rarity, a semi-detached country church.

For a time the house became an inn, the Blue Bell, which was very convenient for officiating clergy. They robed in the pub before services, and no doubt relaxed in it afterwards. They used one of the communicating doors (now blocked up), but if members of the congregation fancied a pint I gather they had to take the long way round.

All Saints' was a 'peculiar' – not because it was semi-detached, but because it owed no allegiance to the bishop of the diocese. The abbot had the authority of a bishop, and when the abbey estate was sold, that authority passed to the landowner who bought it, a Francis Pole. There is a tablet in the church which describes one of Mr Pole's successors, Lord Stanhope, as 'Lay Bishop of Dale', and a later Lord Stanhope took the title so seriously that he installed a 'throne' in what he called his 'cathedral', made from oak trees on his Kent estate.

The throne has gone now, but All Saints' is not short of eccentric furnishings. The altar is a Jacobean cupboard, which stands in front of the reading desk instead of behind it, the congregation can sit in the box pews with their backs to the preacher if they wish, and the pulpit tilts at a most alarming angle

– 'like the Tower of Pisa', as the guidebook frankly admits. A medieval wall-painting shows a young couple on very friendly terms – though the haloes indicate there can be nothing amiss – and even the splendid old font has had a chequered career. It came from the Abbey, but spent some time as a flowerpot-cum-birdbath on the lawns of

nearby Stanton Hall – where I suppose it looked no odder than the gravestones visible from All Saints' windows, in the shared garden of the farmhouse next door.

BELOW The pulpit slopes 'like the Tower of Pisa'; but it is unlikely to fall – there is hardly enough room.

10 miles W of Chesterfield off the A623

Not just 'the plague village' – the sundial can tell you the time in Mexico

EYAM WILL ALWAYS BE KNOWN, whether it likes it or not – and some villagers must feel they are plagued by it – as 'The Plague Village', which voluntarily isolated itself when it was struck by the Great Plague in 1665 to prevent it spreading to other villages. The story has been told yet again in a stained-glass window in St Lawrence's, which was installed as recently as 1985. But the church has many other notable features quite unconnected with that event.

Its wall-paintings, for instance, depict the emblems of the twelve tribes of Israel. Another one is something of a mystery, a skeleton on a gridiron apparently holding a pick and shovel. The gridiron is the emblem of St Lawrence, but why the pick and shovel? Is it a medieval tribute to the local leadminers? Or is it just Old Father Time with a very misshapen scythe? The debate continues.

Then there is the impressive oak chair in the sanctuary, bearing the date 1665 and the name of William Mompesson, the heroic rector who tended his flock during the Plague and saw eighty per cent of them die – including his wife. The chair was rescued by a much later rector from a second-hand shop in Liverpool – and it takes us back to 'The Plague Village' again …

So let's go outside and study the massive and complicated sundial. It not only tells the time in Eyam, but you can work out what it is in places ranging from Mexico to Mecca. Perhaps they were popular holiday spots for Eyam residents in the eighteenth century. From a much earlier age there is the Anglo-Saxon preaching cross, retrieved from the undergrowth by the renowned prison reformer John Howard, no less – I gather he just happened to be passing. And from the present century there is the cricketing gravestone of Harry Bagshaw, who played for Derbyshire and the MCC. It shows the ball hitting the stumps and a figure pointing skywards, indicating not only that his innings is over, but also, one hopes, the direction he took to the pavilion.

There are gravestones with odd errors too, like little Anne Brightmore's, who died 'aged 14 mouths', and Catherine Mompesson's, whose name was spelt wrongly and the final 'o' had to be recut. But perhaps just mentioning it is a grave error in itself, because she was that famous rector's wife – and we are back in 'The Plague Village' again…

RIGHT A cricketer's gravestone has an umpire's finger pointing which way to go.

3 miles W of Chesterfield off the A619

The 63-minute clockface may be embarrassing, but dozing Matilda is too old to care

GAZETTEERS LIKE TO CALL VILLAGES and churches 'timeless', and it has certainly been said of Old Brampton, but St Peter and St Paul's is anything but timeless. In fact it has more time than most – three minutes more in every hour, according to the clock on the south side of the tower. On the face of it, one might say, it looks the same as any other – until you count the divisions between the Roman numerals. Instead of the usual five you will find instances of one or two extra, or one fewer. They all add up to sixty-three minutes instead of the standard sixty.

Local legend has it that the workman painting it had too liquid a lunch at the inn across the road, and returned in cheerful mood. One can only guess if his errors were accidental, or he added the extra minutes just for the hell of it. The church guidebook is no help. When I first visited Brampton in 1991 it made no mention of the clock, which seemed curious; it is after all the oddest feature of St Peter and St Paul's. An oversight, perhaps? But a new guide was published in 1996, with a very readable text and delightful drawings, and it refers to the Norman tower, the addition of the broach spire in the fourteenth century, the stone slabs that roof the porch – but there is no mention of the 63-minute clock. Maybe they just find it embarrassing – but not so embarrassing, I hope, that they decide to repaint it correctly, and spoil all the fun.

The church's other notable feature is the thirteenth-century grave slab, remarkably well preserved, of Matilda Le Caus, a member of the local ruling family. She is depicted almost as if she is lying under the bedclothes, with her head and hands emerging most realistically at one end, and her feet sticking out at the other.

Dozing Matilda has fared rather better than the Revd Thomas Ball, who was vicar of St Peter and St Paul's nearly six hundred years ago. There is an alabaster slab in his memory in the north aisle, but later generations of parishioners do not seem to have been too bothered about it. The 1991 guide mentioned in passing: 'It is partly covered by the cupboards, but is still visible.' The latest guide does not mention it at all.

It does however do full credit to another alabaster monument, to the seventeenth-century Clarke family, a very grand affair 'bursting with life in all its details' – except perhaps for the two skulls at the bottom.

RIGHT Brampton's eccentric clockface – the guidebook is too discreet to mention it, but it has attracted many clockwatchers.

3 miles S of Bakewell off the B5056

A knight in a 'dress', a 'midget' who wasn't, and a much-travelled two-bowl font

ALL SAINTS' IS NOTED FOR ITS SIZE, ITS lofty tower – and its confusing monuments. They range from a medieval knight wearing what one gazetteer calls, alarmingly, a dress, to a three-foot armoured effigy which another guidebook takes at face value and describes as a midget. There is also a Jacobean lady in a tall top-hat (which happened to be the fashion at the time), an alabaster reredos which features the Virgin and Child surrounded by the fifteenth-century Gilbert family – father, mother, seven sons and ten daughters – and a Norman font with a small extra bowl carved out of the same block of stone, not for baptizing exceedingly small babies, but perhaps to hold oil.

The quilted 'dress' worn by Sir John Rossington is actually a gambason, a long doublet which knights wore underneath their armour to stop it scratching. There is no doubt an equally straightforward explanation for the heart he is clutching in both hands, though it is not recorded. Did he normally wear it on his sleeve, and it

BELOW Thomas Cokayne's effigy is only three feet long, but he was no midget; he just died before his father.

slipped? Perhaps not. As for the 'midget', Thomas Cokayne was the usual height, but because he died before his father, his effigy was made smaller. He died in 1488 in a fight with a man called Thomas Burdett, over a disputed marriage settlement.

A nineteenth-century drawing shows him on his table tomb by the chancel door, but something very odd must have happened, because it was discovered in the 1870s in a barn, badly damaged. Perhaps the descendants of Thomas Burdett were having another go. It was beautifully restored and placed in its present prominent position in the centre of the chancel – so perhaps Cokayne had the last laugh after all.

The two-bowl font is described in the guidebook as 'the oldest movable feature in the church', and it has certainly demonstrated its movability. It started life in All Saints' daughter church at Elton. When that church was being rebuilt in the nineteenth century, the font was first moved into the churchyard, then transferred to the vicarage garden at Youlgreave, and finally installed in All Saints'. The parishioners of Elton understandably wanted it back when their church was restored, and offered Youlgreave £5 to make a replica for retaining in All Saints'. Instead, All Saints' kept the font, and Elton got the replica. Daughter churches, presumably had to be kept in their place.

RIGHT The font with the spare bowl, not for baptising very small babies, but perhaps to hold the oil.

8 miles E of Cirencester on the A417

Spot the portraits in the windows, enjoy the misericords – but don't miss Tiddles the cat

ST MARY'S DELIGHTS BOTH THE EXPERTS and the simply curious. It was built by a wealthy cloth merchant, John Tame, at the end of the fifteenth century, and the structure remains unchanged, so the experts relish its late Perpendicular lines and its pinnacles and parapets. The simply curious may be more interested in the tomb of the man responsible. It is in the Lady Chapel, covered by a slab of Purbeck marble. A brass depicts him and his wife, who died nearly thirty years before him and never saw the church built. The inscription says 'For thus love pray for me, I may not pray nowe, pray ye …'. It is tempting to think that in a later age of crisp farewells, J. Tame's epitaph for his wife might have been: 'Je T'aime'.

The experts revel in the windows, twenty-eight of them all, dating from the same period and reckoned to be the finest in such quantity in England. They tell the Christian story from the Creation to the Crucifixion and beyond, with the west window devoted to an awesome Last Judgement, complete with a blue-bearded devil carrying away an old woman to her fate – in a wheelbarrow.

The simply curious can enjoy the windows too, not just because of their quality but also their mystery faces. It is thought that they are actually hidden portraits of royalty and other famous figures of the time. For instance, the king entering the Golden Gates could be Henry VII, the Queen of

RIGHT The Last Judgement window, with St Michael weighing up the saints and the sinners.

Sheba looks like Queen Elizabeth of York, one of the three Wise Men might be the king's heir, Prince Arthur, a foot soldier with Pontius Pilate is definitely a prominent courtier, Sir John Savile (his name is round his neck!) – and so on. At the time they were probably easily recognized by the public; these days there is a helpful leaflet to tell you which is supposed to be whom.

Both the experts and the curious must enjoy the misericords, an entertaining collection ranging from a couple of drunks with a barrel to a lady apparently about to hit a shoe salesman with a ladle – or is the

ABOVE A particularly unpleasant devil's mouth from the Last Judgement window: the lady in the wheelbarrow is there too.

playful fellow just trying to tip her off her chair? Not even the official guide can make up its mind.

But for the really curious, have a look in the churchyard. It is too humble to be mentioned in the church's rather elegant literature, but among the tombstones is a carved stone cat, with the inscription: 'Tiddles the Church Cat, 1963–80'. She was looked after by the verger, who commissioned her memorial. He explained: 'She spent more time in the church than anyone else, and she deserved a plot of her own.' I wonder if the mice thought so too?

LEFT A more humble memorial, to Tiddles the church cat. 'She spent more time in the church than anyone else.'

St Mary the Virgin, Painswick

They may have added a spire – but there'll never be another yew

IN 1632 THE WEALTHY WOOL merchants of Painswick decided to add a lofty spire to the fifteenth-century tower of St Mary's – and some ten years later they had cause to regret it. During the Civil War Charles I chose to stay in the town, and the spire provided an ideal rangefinder for Cromwell's troops. The church still bears the scars of bullets and cannon shots on the walls of the tower and nave.

The spire attracted further misfortune a couple of centuries later when it was struck by lightning in 1883. Forty feet of it fell on to the nave roof and damaged some of the splendid Georgian table tombs in the churchyard. The spire, the roof and the tombs have all been restored, but as it turned out, most visitors are not as interested in the building or the monuments as the church's famous ninety-nine yews.

There are some entertaining stories about these yews, and they always get better with the telling. There is the annual clipping ceremony, for instance, when the uninitiated are led to believe that an army of gardeners with shears and tapemeasures trim the yews into their elegant shapes. But the ceremony dates back to the fourteenth century, and the yews were only planted in 1792. 'Clipping' actually derives from an early English word meaning 'enclose', and traditionally it involves 'enclosing' the church by dancing round it.

The ceremony is combined with Feast

RIGHT The church and some of its ninety-nine yews; they say the Devil would object to a hundred.

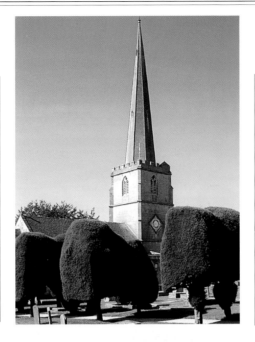

Sunday, when these days children receive a coin and a bun. But according to legend a local landlord ran out of meat for his pies on Feast Sunday, so he killed off some stray dogs and put them in the pies instead. 'Puppy dog pie' became a bizarre annual tradition, but the 'puppies' were only china replicas.

As for the yew trees themselves, romantic souls maintain that the yews which line the path to the church can sometimes be

BELOW The yews spring together 'like bridal couples going to their wedding'.

seen swaying towards each other, like bridal couples and their attendants on the way to their nuptials. There is not too much support for that theory, but the belief has been preserved for centuries that there must only be ninety-nine yews in the churchyard – the Devil, for some reason, would object to a round hundred. So whatever you may think of courting yew trees and puppy-dog pie – it seems fairly certain there'll never be another yew.

LEFT The spire has been restored since it was partially destroyed by lightning.

13 miles NW of Monmouth on the B4347

Cistercians built it 850 years ago
– and a cider-apple grower ensured it had an abbey birthday

DORE ABBEY, FOUNDED IN 1147, IS the only Cistercian abbey in the country that is still in use as a parish church. Only half of the original building now stands, but entering it still gives an amazing impression of vastness, in contrast to the homely wooden porch. It soars above you, with lofty narrow windows extending to the roof; and though the ambulatory now forms the north and south aisles, it is still very easy to visualize the cowled monks walking between its massive sandstone columns.

After the abbey was dissolved in 1536 it passed into the hands of John Scudamore, who demolished the nave and used the revenues to rebuild his house at Holme Lacy. In spite of partially wrecking the abbey, he still had his tomb and effigy in what was left.

In the 1600s his great-grandson Viscount Scudamore, perhaps to make amends, restored the surviving half, the presbytery and transepts, as the parish church. A west wall was built to cut it off from the ruins of the nave and choir, and he engaged the King's Carpenter, John Abel, to repair the roof, provide the furnishings, and make the splendid nave screen. It bears the crests of Charles I, Abel's master, Lord Scudamore, his employer, and Archbishop Laud, who was perhaps the motivating force behind the project.

During the restoration the original stone altar was discovered, not among the ruins but in a farm kitchen, where it was being used for salting meat and pressing cheese. The only damage to it was a chip broken off the front edge, and a piece of wood was fashioned to fit precisely into the gap. It would be nice to think that this was the final touch of the King's Carpenter before he packed up his tools and went back to the palace.

In the midst of all this grandeur there is a comparatively modest tablet to the man responsible – 'the good Lord Scudamore, scholar, diplomat, royalist, benefactor ...' The inscription ends with a reference to his other, lesser-known achievement: 'propagator of Herefordshire's most famous cider apple, the Red Streak, for which let the minster and all ye people thankfully remember him and duly praise God.'

In 1997 Dore Abbey celebrated its 850th anniversary with an exhibition, lectures and special services. I hope there was plenty of cider around, to honour its restorer as well as wish it an abbey birthday.

LEFT AND RIGHT The screen built by the King's Carpenter, with the coat of arms of his master, Charles I, as the central feature.

12 miles W of Hereford on the B4348

Bad news for Thomas à Becket but good news for Dorstone: it got a new church and a pub

WHEN HENRY II CRIED 'WHO WILL rid me of this turbulent priest?' one of the four knights who put up their hands was Richard de Brito. After they assassinated Thomas à Becket, King Henry had his well-known change of heart and sent them off to the Crusades as a penance, no doubt hoping they would not come back. But de Brito survived, and it is said that when he returned, as an additional penance, he built a chapel which became St Faith's – and for good measure, he built the local pub as well.

Very little evidence of de Brito or his family survives in the church, because the Victorians completely rebuilt it – twice. But during the rebuilding they broke into the tomb of Johannes de Brito, a descendant of Richard's who died in 1275. It contained, as well as his bones, an ancient pewter chalice and paten, which are now preserved in the church. They also found pieces of a stone sill from the original church, inscribed in Latin: 'This chapel is dedicated to the Virgin Mary as promised by Richard de Brito 1256.'

Richard would have been long since dead by then, but it suggests the chapel was his idea and perhaps Johannes put the idea into effect, either to carry out his wishes or to restore the family's good name. It would be a neat end to the story if another sill was found which said: 'Incidentally, I built the chapel for Richard – signed, Johannes …'

A less likely legend attached to St Faith's is about a man called Jack de France who saw the Devil there one All Souls' Eve, announcing the names of those who would die in the coming year. One of the names Jack heard was his own: he died of shock.

However, the deaths of five infant children in one family is clearly recorded,

ABOVE The pewter chalice found in the tomb of Johannes de Brito, descendant of an assassin of Becket's who also founded the Pandy In (left).

according to the guidebook, on a tombstone in the churchyard – though I confess I could not find it. They died in the 1850s and their epitaph reads: 'Lifeless infants though they be, you may learn one tip from we. Think whene'er you see this spot, you have sinned but we have not.' 'Learn one tip' in the 1850s? A very down-to-earth stonemason.

Incidentally, Richard de Brito's inn is now called the Pandy, the medieval name for a cloth mill, where weavers thickened their cloth into flannel. But happily a sign by the road still illustrates its earlier origin: it shows Thomas à Becket being murdered on the altar steps in Canterbury Cathedral – and one of those chaps with the swords is Richard de Brito.

8 miles NW of Worcester off the A443

The Venetian-style church which was 'built on nails' – with a ceiling full of surprises

IN THE DAYS OF CROMWELL'S Commonwealth, much of the common wealth of the country passed into the hands of the ironmasters. One of them, Richard Foley, made a fortune out of producing nails, so later generations of his family were able to create a vast mansion at Great Witley and build a splendid church to match it. Unfortunately, a later Foley gambled away the family fortune, the mansion passed into other hands and eventually became a ruin – but the church just beside it still survives, and it is considered by many experts to be the finest Baroque church in the country.

The interior decorations were largely acquired from the sumptuous mansion and chapel of the Duke of Chandos when it was pulled down in 1747. The Foleys bought the organ, the ten painted glass windows, and the ceiling decorations by the noted Venetian Antonio Bellucci – three large paintings and some twenty smaller ones. The ceiling is not only magnificent but full of surprises. One of the many cherubs is a Down's Syndrome child – perhaps because they were regarded by many as 'God's special children'. Another cherub is less easy to explain: it apparently has two bottoms. The most unusual feature, though, is the 'stucco' mouldings – which in fact are papier-mâché.

It may seem an odd material to use in a church ceiling, and indeed this is the first recorded instance of its use in England,

but it does have considerable advantages. Stonework can crumble, wood can rot, glass can break and iron can rust, but papier-mâché can go on and on – unless of course it gets wet. And this has been one of the extra problems in restoring and preserving St Michael and All Angels, as well as protecting the paintings and fending off dry rot, death-watch beetle and all the other usual hazards. One antiquarian has said he wished all parish churches in the country were as handsome as this, but I suspect few parishes knowing the cost of its upkeep would agree.

Rebuilding the church in this style, linked with a mansion like a private chapel was the idea of the first Lord Foley, great-grandson of the nail manufacturer, but he did not live to see it materialize. Nevertheless he has the biggest monument in the church, depicting him as a leisurely Roman, lolling elegantly on one elbow. If he had wished to commemorate where all the money came from to build the monument and the church, he might have been depicted on a bed of nails; but understandably he prefers the Roman equivalent of a sofa.

RIGHT The ceiling may look magnificent, but the decorations are papier-mâché – its earliest recorded use in England.

12 miles W of Hereford on the B4348

An ancient altar which may go back to King Arthur – and above it, a fibreglass spire

MOST OF ST PETER'S IS SEVEN or eight hundred years old, and it has some fine original Norman arches, but there is one feature believed to be much older, and another which is definitely much younger, even though it may not look it at first glance.

Inside the Norman sanctuary, which has a rather disconcerting blue ceiling studded with stars, there is a stone altar believed to have been brought down from a Neolithic burial ground on nearby Dorstone Hill, which later presumably became a site of Christian worship. Like so many hilltop sites in this locality, it is called Arthur's Stone: who knows? In accordance with ancient tradition, the altar has five little crosses carved on it, one in the centre and the others at each corner.

While the age of the altar has to be guessed at, there is no doubt about the date of St Peter's spire – though the material it is made of may come as a surprise. The original spire became unsafe and was taken down in 1949, and during the next two decades various materials were suggested for a replacement, ranging from aluminium to pre-stressed concrete. The final choice was fibreglass – referred to discreetly in the local guide as 'modern material' – and in 1972 the

prefabricated spire, over a hundred feet high and a landmark throughout the Golden Valley, was hoisted into position in three sections by a giant crane. There was a nasty moment when the top section failed to fit, but the vicar took it philosophically. 'No one has done a job like this before, and we are meeting problems as they come,' he is quoted as saying. The problem was met – and overcome. Unfortunately the spire's steel supports are now showing signs of needing repair, and the old argument has re-opened.

Another unusual feature of St Peter's is its chained trout. This handsome fish is preserved in a glass case on the wall opposite the door, probably the first thing to catch the visitor's eye, and it looks rather reminiscent of a fishing trophy over the bar of a pub – except that it has a chain around its neck.

The fish is a plaster cast of one which is said to have been caught in the nearby River Dore. When it was reeled in it was found to be wearing a gold chain. The chain may have been dropped into the water accidentally and the fish became entangled with it, but more likely it is intended to be allegorical, epitomizing St Peter the Fisherman *ad vincula* – in chains.

Whatever its origins, it is undoubtedly a very fine fish.

LEFT A chained trout in plaster by the door; was it caught like that, or is it in honour of St Peter the Fisherman?
RIGHT The fibreglass spire on top of a medieval tower provides a striking landmark throughout the Golden Valley.

12 miles SW of Hereford off the A465

The cocks, the keys and the upside-down saint
– a case of 'attractive indulgence'?

VISITORS TO ROWLSTONE CHURCH can be in no doubt about the identity of its patron saint. St Peter held the Keys of Heaven, and was unhappily associated with a cock crowing thrice – everywhere in and around St Peter's you are liable to find keys and cocks.

Outside the church there is the obvious cock on the weathervane, on top of the pyramid roof of the sixteenth-century tower. There are cocks and keys on the big churchyard cross, and as you enter the south door, on each side of the tympanum above it portraying Christ in Majesty, not uncommon over church doors, there are the ubiquitous birds on the capitals.

Inside, the nave has a kind of dado running along the wall, and of course it carries a cock motif. When it reaches the Norman chancel arch, dating back to the twelfth century, the final cock on each side is alongside St Peter and his guardian angel. On the south side, however, while the cock is looking as upright and perky as ever, St Peter and his friend are mysteriously upside-down.

According to the church guide, 'this is popularly supposed to represent St Peter crucified downwards' – but where is the cross, and why should his angel have to be upside-down too? I prefer the educated guess of the great authority Pevsner, who reckons it was just carelessness by the stonemason – and his master let it go. 'Such indulgence is attractive,' says Pevsner. It also provides a conundrum for the experts to argue about in later centuries.

The final flock of cocks is roosting in the chancel itself, on a most unusual candle bracket. It is nearly five feet long, and pivots on a hinge on the wall. Along the lower bar are five little spikes, or prickets, on which to put the candles. Perched on the bar above them are six cocks, one behind the other – and perhaps feeling a little uncomfortable when the candles are lit.

There is an identical bracket on the opposite wall, except the birds look more like swans than cocks. But why swans, one wonders? Perhaps this is another case of what Pevsner called 'attractive indulgence': the craftsman who made the bracket wasn't very good at doing cocks, this was the nearest he could get – and his master let it go.

BELOW Some of the cocks which have found their way into St Peter's. They are perched along a candle bracket in the chancel.

Death by sorcery, an earl and countess under the table – and a case for Cadfael?

'THE WITCHCRAFT TOMB' IS THE ONE that most visitors head for in St Mary's, the only tomb in the country with an inscription referring to children's deaths by sorcery. Actually it is an impressive tomb in its own right, so lofty that the chancel roof had to be made higher, and even then a rafter was partially cut away to take the peacock crest on top.

The tomb had to be that high to accommodate the lengthy inscription. It refers mainly to the sixth Earl of Rutland, who lies there between his two countesses, but it also mentions his two sons, 'who died in their infancy by wicked practice and sorcery'. It seems the earl's family fell foul of the Belvoir Witches, three local harridans who were blamed for the earl and countess suffering convulsions, and for the subsequent deaths of their two sons. The women were convicted of murder in 1618; one died during the trial and the other two were hanged.

However, this is only one of the twelve imposing tombs of the de Roos and Manners families of Belvoir Castle which fill the chancel, and others have interesting features too. For instance, the second earl and his wife are depicted lying underneath a dining table. That might prompt unkind assumptions about their life-style, but more probably the tomb represents a Communion table.

The effigy with the most mysterious

RIGHT One of the Earl of Rutland's sons 'who died in their infancy by wicked practice and sorcery'.

story is not among the grand collection in the chancel, but in a far corner at the back of the church. It is known as the Fair Maid of Normanton, though the face is now quite featureless. Legend has it that she was a young member of the de Roos household at the castle who acquired such a lurid reputation that, after her death, successive earls and dukes refused to allow her effigy inside the church until 1905 – hence its weatherbeaten appearance – and then only in an obscure corner.

Interestingly, an old register records the burial of a young woman who had been found dead in a Normanton field, and there is also a tale of yet another woman who died from a blow on the skull while playing ball on Shrove Tuesday – and earwigs came out of her head! One wonders, was the disgraced de Roos girl disposed of by a family servant and hidden in the field, only to be discovered years later – full of earwigs – and the ball-game story was invented as a cover-up? Perhaps Brother Cadfael could have unravelled the answer.

LEFT The Fair Maid of Normanton, not quite so fair after being kept outside the church for centuries.

RIGHT The other infant son of the Earl of Rutland. The skulls had no connection with witchcraft, they indicate the children died early.

7 miles S of Oakham off the A6003

One bishop compromised about keeping on the rails; the other went up the wall

ST ANDREW'S HAS TWO UNUSUAL reminders of two unusual bishops who were separated by 350 years. The first was the seventeenth-century Bishop Williams of Lincoln, in the days when his diocese covered this part of Rutland. At that time traditional churchmen wanted to retain the altar against the east wall, but reformers wanted them in the middle of the chancel or nave, so they could be more conveniently used as Communion tables. In 1634, to stop all the arguments and create uniformity, Archbishop Laud ordered that altars must stay at the east end of the church and be railed off.

Bishop Williams, however, did not agree with Laud and devised a compromise. He decreed that in his diocese altars should indeed be at the east end, but not against the wall; and there should be a rail, but it would extend around all four side of the altar. St Andrew's is one of the very few churches which retains this evidence of the bishop's cunning ploy.

The much later Bishop of Peterborough, known to millions of 'Thought for the Day' listeners on Radio 4 as Bill Westwood, has, appropriately, a more easily understood memorial. To mark the 450th anniversary in 1991 of the founding of the diocese – and as it happened, the 110th anniversary of Lyddington being absorbed in it – a master mason was engaged to carve a replica of Bill's head. It adorns one wall of the church, facing a Green Man, representing the Diocese of Lincoln, on the wall opposite. As always the bishop is wearing spectacles – but again, as always, one can detect the twinkle in the eyes behind them.

Another wall decoration is not so easy to recognize. Six earthenware jars were incorporated into the wall on each side of the chancel in the fifteenth century, but they lie horizontally and at ninety degrees to the wall, with only their mouths visible. Apparently they represent the earliest form of acoustic equipment, first used in Greek and Roman theatres to amplify the voices of the actors, and adopted for a similar purpose in some churches throughout Europe to give the priest's voice more resonance in the sanctuary. Those at St Andrew's are among the rare survivors. They may not be as effective as microphones and loudspeakers, but they are a lot more discreet.

BELOW AND RIGHT An earlier bishop put the rails around the altar; Bishop Bill Westwood is carved on the wall, perhaps permanently pondering on the next Thought for the Day.

4 miles S of Oakham on the A6003

Gethsemane cypresses, Nicosia marble, and lamps from 'The Street called Straight'

ST PETER AND ST PAUL'S IS A TRADITIONAL English country church – as befits Preston, 'a priest's village'. The original Saxon building has gone, but this one dates back eight hundred years or more – the massive circular pillars, for instance, were built about 1150. The chancel was remodelled in the thirteenth century, and the clerestory windows were installed about a century later. All the early English architectural styles are represented, from the Decorated to the Tudor.

And yet, on close inspection, the church has a number of Middle Eastern touches. The most obvious examples are the hanging brass lamps in the sanctuary, which could well have come straight from the Arabian Nights. Actually they come from 'The Street which is called Straight' in Damascus,

and do did the two tall brass candlesticks beneath them.

Then there are the fragments of marble in the floor on each side of the chancery steps: they came from the mosaic pavement of St John the Baptist Church in Constantinople. In the face of the steps is a piece of serpentine marble from St Sophia's Church in Nicosia, and an alms box comes from a church in Asia Minor.

In the churchyard a little notice under the cypress trees gives a clue to how these unlikely items came to be here. It explains that the trees were grown from seed brought home in 1925 from the Garden of Gethsemane by the rector, the Revd John Codrington.

The Codrington family were great benefactors of the church, but, perhaps

fortunately, they were not all so interested in the Middle East. They donated, for instance, two of the church bells. One is inscribed 'Alfred E. Codrington gave me, 1908', the other was given in 1964 by the family of William Codrington. The most striking gift – in a different sense from the bells – is the set of abstract stained-glass windows in the chancel, donated by Col. John Codrington.

In their own way they are just as untraditional as the brass lamps and the fragments of mosaic – but when the Norman builders of St Peter and St Paul's used alternate courses of ironstone and Ketton stone to give the walls grey and orange stripes, no doubt they were thought rather odd too …

BELOW The lamps in the sanctuary could have come straight out of the Arabian Nights.

5 miles N of Corby on the A6003

No plotters, no witch – just St Edmund being shot by American Indians

FIRST THE BAD NEWS, IF YOU ENJOY A good legend. There are two attached to the priest's room over the north porch at St Andrew's. The first is that Sir Everard Digby hosted the secret meeting in this room which planned the Gunpowder Plot – and indeed there are monuments to Sir Everard's ancestors and family all over the church, but not Sir Everard's itself – he was hanged for his part in the Plot. The second and more lurid legend concerns a rector who in medieval times sealed up a witch in this room and starved her to death.

Alas, both stories have been firmly quashed by one of that rector's more down-to-earth successors. A notice on the door says firmly that the legends 'cannot be supported'. It points out that, although Sir Everard was Lord of the Manor for a time,

he married an heiress and moved into her house in Bucks, making over the Stoke Dry estate to his son, years before the Gunpowder Plot. Wherever he did his plotting, it was not in this room. As for the sealed-up witch, she does not merit a further mention – just an exclamation mark …

However, the good news is that St Andrew's offers other material for the legend-lover. It is pointed out, for instance, that the Digby Chapel was invisible from the nave, so the Catholic Digbys could hold discreet services in it, with the priest's door offering an emergency exit if required.

The most dramatic legend is illustrated by one of the thirteenth-century wall-paintings in the chantry chapel. As well as the familiar portrayal of St Christopher carrying the boy Jesus, there is a scene showing St Edmund being shot full of arrows, not by the usual Danes, but what look like American Indians – feather head-dresses and all. It has been taken as confirmation that the Vikings did discover America 200 years before Columbus. Indeed one American visitor claimed he recognised the tribe.

Just one more: on one of the Norman pillars supporting the chancel arch is a man pulling a bell-rope, with a figure grovelling below which is thought to be the Devil, stricken by the sound of the Sanctus bell. On the other hand, it might just be a neighbour, driven mad by the noise. Either way, could it be the earliest representation of a bell-ringer on a pillar? It's worth a try.

LEFT AND RIGHT St Edmund apparently being shot dead by American Indians, and perhaps the earliest appearance of a bellringer.

11 miles NW of Lincoln off the B1241

Heraldic Designers with a Penchant for Puns – in a Church with a Rood Surprise

MANY COUNTRY CHURCHES HAVE winding stone stairs at the chancel arch, leading up to where the rood loft used to be, but very few still have the loft itself. St Edith's has the most complete medieval rood screen and loft in Lincolnshire, and probably far beyond that. It is an astonishing find in such a remote little church by a lonely farmhouse – and the guidebook suggests it was this remoteness that saved it when other rood lofts were being ripped down as idolatrous, because they bore the figures of the Crucifixion. However, at St Edith's the figures were not standing on the loft itself but were painted on the boarding above it, and nearly all that has been destroyed and replaced by plain timber - so it was not as remote as all that.

The screen was restored in the 1880s to look much as it did in medieval times, and so indeed was the rest of the church - the architect, J L Pearson, was not as heavy-handed as most of his contemporaries. He moved out the Georgian box pews, restored the fifteenth-century bench pews (which look authentically uncomfortable), and retrieved the original medieval pulpit from a nearby barn, to substitute it for a later two-decker.

In its early years St Edith's was virtually the family chapel of the local squires, the Butlers. At that time Coates had a population of twenty; it is even smaller today, just the farm and a few cottages. So the Butlers, who owned the village between the 1560s and 1673, have their memorials in all the prime positions. One brass depicts Charles Butler, his wife (called Douglass, confusingly) and their eight children, three of whom carry skulls to show they died before their parents. Another depicts his brother William with his wife and their only child, who died as a baby and is wrapped in swaddling clothes. The most imposing monument is not to a Butler but a Cooke – who was a relation of the Butlers.

Incidentally the Butler arms featured three cups, as carried by butlers, and the arms of the Tyrwhit family - Douglass was a Tyrwhit - featured peewits, known as 'tirrets' in Lincolnshire. With their penchant for puns, the heraldic designers would have had no problems with Mr Cooke …

A less prominent tomb slab commemorating the Hansard family 'covers the body of a horse, according to an inexplicable local legend', says the guidebook. But it is not entirely inexplicable. Whether it was carved on the original inscription, or is just a quirk of how it has been worn by time, I could distinctly make out the head of a horse. Can the punsters explain that, I wonder? Is the answer somewhere in Hansard?

LEFT The medieval rood screen still has its loft intact, one of the few such combinations to survive. The original pulpit was retrieved from a barn.

7 miles S of Grantham off the A1

Newton's bust is honoured with an apple – but his sundial is upside-down behind the organ

WHEN THE NORMANS REBUILT THE original church of St John the Baptist they found the Saxons had selected a sloping site, and so the pillars had to be custom-built to fit. There is a difference of over two feet between the heights of the pillars at each end of the nave, in order to make the roof level. It was an exercise which may have fascinated a later worshipper in the church, Sir Isaac Newton. With his scientific mind he may have whiled away a boring sermon by working out how they did it.

Even as a boy he enjoyed such calculations. 'He was diligent in observing the motion of the sun,' wrote one biographer. As a result St John's has a complex little sundial which he carved with a penknife on a wall at his home, Woolsthorpe Manor, when he was only nine. It is a confusing sundial, not only because it has been put on the inside wall of the church, instead of the outside like most church sundials, but also because it has been installed upside-down. So to give the time, the sunlight would have to fall upwards, thus defying his own laws of gravity. As it happens, it never sees any sunlight: it is now almost completely concealed behind the organ.

Newton is rather better commemorated by a bust in the north aisle, with other memorabilia. Here again there is an unusual feature. While other memorials are often kept supplied with fresh flowers, Newton's bust is kept supplied with a fresh apple, an apt reminder of how it was a falling apple, according to legend, which started him off.

Much of the church remains as he would have known it, but the chancel was completely rebuilt in the 1870s by the Revd John Mirehouse to replace the 'hideous barn-like construction' that had been built a century before. The philanthropic rector also gave, among other items, the seven-branched brass candlestick, a copy of the one in the Tabernacle in Jerusalem and said to be the only one of its kind in the country.

The east window portraying the Last Supper is in memory of Mrs Thomas Ord, wife of another rector, who has another memorial window in the tower room. As the church guide observes: 'The lady is therefore in the unique position of having the praise of two memorials, one at each end of the church.'

Not even Sir Isaac Newton, with his sundial hidden behind the organ, can quite match that.

LEFT AND RIGHT Sir Isaac Newton does not have flowers laid before his bust, he gets a symbolic apple. He also appears behind the organ, and in this case he has a sundial, which he carved on a wall when he was nine.

12 miles NE of Sleaford on the A153

A rogue monkey, a tragic flag, Britannia with wings – and of course, that clock

MANY VISITORS TO ST MICHAEL'S just come to see its enormous one-handed clock – and indeed they can hardly miss it. The face is 16 ½ feet across, said to be the largest of its kind in the country, if not the world. It has to be wound up every day; I have tried it, and it is like cranking a very stubborn tractor. So when the mechanism became so worn some years back that it finally stopped, one might have thought it was a good opportunity to replace it with a modern clock – with two hands. There was such an outcry, the old one was restored – and you still have to guess at the minutes.

But there are other interesting features at St Michael's, some with tragic tales to tell. Over the south porch, for example, is a stone monkey, recalling the unhappy fate of the infant Viscount Coningsby in 1733. The three-month-old baby was stolen from its cradle by the family's pet monkey, and when the nurse tried to catch it, the monkey climbed to the top of the house and dropped the baby to the ground. It died instantly; there is no record of what happened to the monkey.

There is another sad story, from a more modern age, behind the Dutch flag in the RAF Chapel, dedicated to the men who flew from Coningsby during the war. One of them was shot down over Holland and hidden with other aircrew by a sixty-year-old Resistance worker, Jacoba Pulskens. They were found by the Nazis and shot on the spot. Jacoba was arrested but before being taken away – later to die in a concentration camp – she draped this flag over their bodies. After the war it was given to St Michael's for safe keeping.

However, nobody knows the significance of the Britannia-like figure with wings on a shelf near the north door. She stands over a kneeling knight, beneath the word 'Coningsby'. Had she flown in to meet St George before he took on the dragon? Or had he already defeated it and she is saying: 'Well done; come and celebrate in Coningsby'?

There are questions too about one of the many carved heads in the church. It has some kind of strap or mask over its mouth. Could the mason have been to the Crusades, seen Moorish women in veils and thought it a nice idea? The more expert opinion is that this is one of just a dozen such heads in the country, portraying a scold's bridle, the medieval punishment for nagging wives. Perhaps the mason suffered from the same problem, and this was just a little wishful thinking …

LEFT AND RIGHT A scold's bridle, perhaps wishful thinking by the henpecked mason, and the clock that tells the time one-handed.

7 miles N of Peterborough on the A1073

A sermon in stone, an en-suite font – and a lonely figure sitting on the bridge

CROYLAND ABBEY – AS IT IS STILL known, even though the village's name has devolved into Crowland – had a very rough ride during its pre-parish church days, from the laying of its foundation stone by King Ethelbald in AD 716 until its dissolution by Henry VIII. It was plundered by the Danes, rebuilt, accidentally burnt down, rebuilt, destroyed by an earthquake, rebuilt, burnt down again in 1143, and rebuilt. After that the accident-prone abbey did rather better – until along came Henry VIII's commissioners, and most of it was reduced to ruins, leaving the great west front with its splendid statues, and the nave and two aisles to serve as the parish church.

Even after that its troubles continued. Cromwell's men bombarded it during a three-month siege, and in the 1700s the nave roof collapsed, and the south aisle was dismantled to provide stone for sealing off the north aisle, which is the present church. Even that was in danger of collapse in the last century, but an energetic rector wrote seventeen thousand letters and appeals, and raised the necessary money to save it – assisted, no doubt, by its three patron saints, St Mary, St Guthlac who first settled on the site, and St Bartholomew, who came to his aid when he had problems with the locals. Up until then, perhaps, they had all been looking the other way …

Even in its reduced state the church looks enormously impressive – and it has some unusual features. At the west end there are high railings round each corner: visitors are sometimes told – only jokingly – that unfaithful wives were put behind them, but they actually protected the clock weights which used to hang there. A stone slab has a full-size figure of the mason who built the vaulted ceiling, holding the Masonic compass and set-square. They are a sermon in stone: 'keep within what your means can encompass – and live squarely'. And beside it, set into a pillar, is what looks like a massive holy water stoup but is actually an en-suite Norman font.

The abbey's strangest relic, which used to be on its roof, now sits on the three-way bridge in Crowland, which once spanned three streams. Experts think it may be King Ethelbald holding his orb, or Christ holding the world. To me it has always looked like a forlorn traveller, waiting for a boat that will never come, along a river that no longer exists. And if he has to wait much longer, he'll open that lunch-box he has been holding so long.

BELOW This 'en-suite font' is carved into a church pillar, unlike the standard free-standing variety.

10 miles NW of Lincoln on the B1241

St Etheldreda may not have planted her staff here, but Lady Godiva certainly lent a hand

THE EARLY HISTORY OF THE ANCIENT Saxon Minster of St Mary's is so bound up with myth and legend it is difficult to sort out which is which, but the guidebook does its best. It contradicts, for example, a 'misleading' brass plate on a damaged arch in the church, which says the damage was caused by the Danes in 870 – the church was not built until a century later. The plate also suggests that Stow was the ancient Sidnacester, seat of the old Bishopric of Lindsey before the Danish invasions – 'a theory now generally not accepted', says the guidebook coldly.

It is also not happy about the legend that St Etheldreda planted her ash staff on the site of the church and it miraculously burst into leaf. It does not deny the miracle, but says it may well have happened at quite a different Stow.

So what did happen at this Stow? Apparently the Saxon bishops of Dorchester-on-Thames owned the area, and in about 975 Bishop Aelfnoth built a head minster here for this part of his large diocese, giving rise to the tradition that St Mary's was the mother church of Lincoln Cathedral. When that church was largely destroyed by fire it was rebuilt by another Saxon bishop, with a generous endowment from Earl Leofric of Mercia and his persuasive wife, Lady Godiva. Some of that church still stands, and so does the nave built by the first Norman bishop of Dorchester. The guidebook adds cautiously: 'many historians and scholars might well disagree with parts of this account', but I'll buy it.

The remarkable appearance of St Mary's cannot be disputed. It is a venerable mixture of Saxon, Norman and Gothic – there are windows of all three periods in just one group on the south chancel – and its atmosphere inside is still cathedral-like. In the last century it became so dilapidated it was nearly replaced by a smaller, more convenient building, but an energetic Rector raised the money to have it restored to its original appearance.

His successors have sometimes wondered if it was the right decision – there is a big empty gap between congregation and chancel, and the pulpit's position, literally on the end of the front pew, is singularly impractical – but the rest of us must be thankful, particularly the archaeologists, if only for the scratched picture of an oared sailing ship on a pier in the chancel. It is the earliest known representation in England of a Viking ship.

BELOW Three periods of window in one wall: Saxon, Norman and Gothic.

2 miles S of Birkenhead on the B5136

He built a church which was roomy, warm and comfortable - but he couldn't see the clock

ALL SAINTS' IS THAT CONTRADICTION in several terms, a Gothic Early English church built in the nineteenth century. It was the creation of the wealthy Yorkshire wool merchant Joseph Hirst, who acquired a country residence in the vicinity and became a benefactor to the village. He built the church, the vicarage and the church school, and threw in an endowment of £1,000 to help them along. At the consecration service in 1868, according to the *Birkenhead News & Adver-tiser*: 'The inhabitants availed themselves fully of the opportunity to show the feeling they entertained for one who, though a stranger to these parts, has in such a Christian and liberal spirit provided for the spiritual and educational needs of the district.'

Mr Hirst did not skimp. He built All Saints' big enough to take 460 people. The pulpit, desk and altar rail were made of oak 'elaborately carried out'. The font and the reredos, depicting the Last Supper, were of Caen stone. Perhaps more importantly to the congregation – and more rarely in country churches – he installed an efficient central heating system, though there were also elaborate ventilating arrangements 'for the emission of vitiated air'. Equally importantly, the pews were designed 'in a form perfectly easy to the occupants'. The only personal feature was a stained-glass window of the Crucifixion in memory of his only daughter Mary, who died in childbirth a year after her marriage.

The whole project cost about £8,500, a modest fortune in those days. It has since been rather overshadowed by his successor, Lord Leverhulme, who rebuilt the rest of the village in picturesque Tudor, complete with a village smithy under the inevitable chestnut tree, but at the time it made an enormous impact. At a tea party for parishioners after the service, in a marquee - provided of course by Mr Hirst – he was presented with a silver tray worth a hundred guineas, itself no mean gift from a small village, in recognition of his generosity. The church was built in just over a year; as the *Advertiser* commented: 'Mr Hirst exercises great promptitude in whatever he takes in mind.'

In this case, though, he may have been a little too prompt. When it was finished, he found the church clock was out of sight from his home because of the intervening roof. Lesser men might have muttered a curse or kicked the cat, but Mr H did not get where he was by cursing or cat-kicking; he just paid for an extra clockface above the existing one, where he could see it - and the two faces have been ticking away in tandem ever since.

LEFT Jospeh Hirst spent a small fortune building a church, then found the clock was out of sight. This was his solution.

6 miles N of Northampton on the A508

Most of the mysteries are too old to solve – unless this is where St Boniface lost his voice

ALL SAINTS' IS ONE OF THOSE RARE churches which baffle all the experts. They know it was built in the seventh or eighth century, and it is the biggest building in the country to survive from that period. But why was it built so big, and who could afford to build it? Where did all the Roman tiles come from that were used in its arches? And how did it survive so intact over all these centuries, through Danish invasions, the Norman Conquest, the Reformation and the Civil War – not to mention the Victorian restorers?

There are many theories, but nobody really knows, which helps to make All Saints' such a remarkable church – that, and of course its age. Features which would be considered ancient in most churches, like the Saxon spiral staircase on the outside of the tower and the Norman arch over the main door, are comparatively modern by All Saints' standards. The staircase is two or three hundred years later than the tower it was tacked on to, and the Norman arch is five hundred years later than the original one above it - which is composed of Roman tiles that are three or four hundred years older than that.

Compared with these surroundings the oldest effigy in the church, believed to be the tomb of the thirteenth-century Sir John de Verdun who built the Lady Chapel, is quite a recent addition. However, there is one much older relic, which used to be on a shelf beside the pulpit but is now kept more securely. It was found in a hole in the wall of the Lady Chapel early in the last century. A wooden box contained a piece of fabric wrapped round a small piece of bone, which was identified as part of a human larynx.

On the box were the initials TB, and the last chantry priest in the sixteenth century was Thomas Bassenden. So it may have been his box, which perhaps he hid for safety – but it certainly wasn't his bone. The popular theory is that it was a relic of St Boniface, because there are references in church documents to Guilds of St Boniface, and there were festivities around St Boniface's Day on June 5th. But he was born in Devon and was martyred in Germany; so how did his larynx bone get to Brixworth?

But perhaps evidence will come to light that he spent a holiday in Northamptonshire, and mysteriously lost his voice. That would be one less mystery to solve.

BELOW The impressive interior of All Saints', the biggest building of its era still surviving.

6 miles S of Wellingborough off A509

An aisleful of the Yelvetons' rampant lions, but the literary lions were there too

EASTON MAUDIT WAS YELVETON country for centuries, and St Peter and St Paul's is still very much a Yelveton church. The family takes up quite a bit of room one way and another, and their coats of arms with the three rampant lions are very much in evidence. The four hatchments in the north aisle, for instance, were all connected with the last Yelvetons, who were Earls of Sussex. With them are a helm, a sword, a gauntlet and banners, which all probably belonged to the third earl, who died in 1799. It may seem curious equipment for that period, but the earl would never have actually used them in anger; they would just have been carried symbolically at his funeral.

The Victorians thinned out the Yelveton monuments, but there are still two massive ones. Sir Christopher, who bought Easton Maudit in 1578, lies beside his wife Mary. He was made Speaker of the House of Commons, an office which by tradition is reluctantly received, but Sir Christopher sounded more reluctant than most. 'My stature is small, myself not so well spoken, my nature bashful, my purse thin …' But he got the job.

Near by, with a monument extending from floor to ceiling, is his son Henry, apparently lolling in a library with his wife. The books on the shelves, confusingly, are all back to front, so the titles are not shown. This was not because they were a little risqué, or the stonemason was taking a short cut; it seems to have been the custom in those days. Presumably you had to memorize where each one was. The monument has all the emblems of mortality which sculptors like to include when they had a whole wall to fill, and in the midst of them, incongruously, there are Sir Christopher's favourite spectacles. Let's hope he remembers where he left them, once he has found the right book …

The literary flavour is reflected by a brass plaque on one of the front pews. It records that David Garrick, Dr Johnson and Oliver Goldsmith all worshipped in the church. They were friends of an eighteenth-century rector, Thomas Percy, who was a man of letters himself. He compiled and edited *Reliques of Ancient Poetry* at Easton Maudit, verses and ballads from Chaucer to Charles I. It brought him lasting fame, but it narrowly escaped disaster before it was even published. A housemaid was about to light a fire with the original manuscript when Dr Percy, perhaps with Divine guidance, wandered into the room and spotted her in time. I reckon that deserves a brass plaque too.

BELOW The brass plaque records that three of a former rector's famous friends worshipped here: Garrick, Dr Johnson and Oliver Goldsmith RIGHT Henry Yelveton and his wife loll in the library. The books are back to front, so you have to guess the titles.

7 miles SE of Corby off the A6116

The rebuilding of the church by Sir Henry Greene 'was probably curtailed by his execution'

'LOWICK', SAYS THE CHURCH LEAFLET enthusiastically, 'is one of the finest medieval churches in England' – and from then on, the enthusiasm seldom falters. The monument to Sir Ralph Greene and his wife, dated 1420, 'is one of the finest of its period in the country'. The memorial to his descendant the Earl of Wiltshire 'is one of the finest pieces of fifteenth-century carving known'. His tomb chest bears an effigy 'which must be the finest one of its date in existence'. The leaflet deserves one of its own superlatives: 'one of the most enthusiastic almost anywhere …'

But the enthusiasm is well placed; the monuments are magnificent. Beside Ralph Greene's tomb is a copy of the order placed for it with the Chellaston alabaster quarries in Derbyshire. It specifies the design of the two reclining figures, with Ralph's right gauntlet gallantly removed so he can hold his wife's hand. The only jarring features are the initials and names carved into the alabaster by childish visitors —few of whom, I suspect, were children. And there is more serious damage too. The monument to the fifth Duke of Dorset portrays him with an angel holding a text, and the angel has one wing broken off – 'one of the subjects of an act of vandalism perpetrated in 1971',

explains the leaflet, its enthusiasm temporarily stifled.

The chapel in which the duke's and other monuments are placed was rebuilt in the fifteenth century by Henry Greene, when he founded a chantry for two priests to pray for him and his family. In particular he may have had in mind his forbear Sir Henry Greene, who started to rebuild the nave and aisles a century before. The rebuilding, says the invaluable leaflet, 'was probably curtailed by the execution of Sir Henry by King Henry IV'. It certainly couldn't have helped.

St Peter's has many other notable memorials, ranging from the son of the first Earl of Peterborough, who died in 1625 aged just eighty-two days, to Lady Betty Germain, who died in 1769 aged eighty-seven years; she survived her husband by half a century.

The most striking feature of St Peter's outside is its profusion of pinnacles, a dozen of them on top of the tower. They are said to represent the twelve disciples, but local legend has it that there were only a few to start with, and that a past rector added one every time his wife had another baby. As the leaflet, in its superlative fashion, might have said: 'Lowick has one of the tallest towers – and one of the tallest stories to go with it ...'

LEFT AND RIGHT The cluster of twelve pinnacles on top of the 95-foot tower may represent the apostles, but the other theory is better.

3 miles NW of Kettering off the A6

Why were half-ton coffin covers in the tower roof?
And whose were those two thousand skulls?

OLY TRINITY IS THE LONGEST church in the county, but it used to be longer and wider. In the 1200s it was owned by Cirencester Abbey, which was wealthy enough to enlarge it on a much grander scale than Rothwell required. After the Reformation some of it fell down, the two transepts were pulled down, and in 1660 lightning knocked off its spire. These days the spire is alongside the tower instead of on top, reminiscent of the famous ghost with its head tucked underneath its arm. It does protect the belfry stairs, but even so it must feel rather ignominious. At least if it is struck again, it won't have so far to fall.

In Victorian times the church was still dilapidated – they kept the local fire engine in the chancel – but major restoration at the turn of the century put matters right, at a cost equivalent to a million pounds today. During later repairs in 1981, two thirteenth-century stone coffin covers, now in the church, were found in the tower roof; it took a special crane and £600 to get them down. No one knows how they got up there, or why.

But this was not the strangest discovery. Much earlier, in 1700, a gravedigger 'suddenly found himself precipitated into a dark abyss', and discovered not just a skeleton in a cupboard but two thousand skulls, some white, some grey, with thighbones to go with them in an old bone crypt. Skulls and thighbones were not just connected with pirates: it used to be thought they were the bones required for the Resurrection. The whiter skulls were older, buried only in shrouds and easily accessible to worms; the grey ones were buried later in coffins, allowing longer for the skin to putrefy on to the bone (just in case this kind of thing fascinates you).

There were various theories about their origin: victims of the Black Death, perhaps, or casualties from the Battle of Naseby. But there were more skulls than battle casualties, and indeed more than the entire population of Rothwell – and the dates were wrong anyway. It seems they were just local residents who died between the fourteenth and sixteenth centuries. Some were probably dug up during the extensions to the church, others much later when Jesus Hospital was built in 1591, and they were all just tossed into the crypt.

I made one more discovery at Rothwell, minor by comparison but fascinating to me. The records of the Overseers of the Poor for 1785 revealed the item: 'For a pare of britches for old Timson, 2s. 3d.' So that's where these old slacks came from …

LEFT The bone crypt contains two thousand skulls, and the thighbones to go with them.

1 mile E of Corby off the A427

The lantern windows used to help travellers: now they come to see the windows below

THERE IS NO MISTAKING ST MARY'S. It is not uncommon for seaside churches to have some kind of beacon as a guide to mariners, but Weldon is about as far inland as you can get, yet St Mary's has a glass cupola on top of its tower, containing a lantern. It was a guide, not to seafarers but to treefarers …

It dates back to when Weldon-in-the-Woods really was in the woods, surrounded by Rockingham Forest. It was not all woodland, but there was enough to get lost in, and legend has it that one lost traveller only found his way out when he spotted St Mary's tower. That was presumably in daylight, but he realized a light would be invaluable – and donated it. Normally the glass windows of the cupola only reflect the light instead of providing it; the more interesting windows these days are down in the church below.

One of the oldest is a sixteenth-century Flemish window in the tower portraying the Nativity, with Mary and her Child as the centrepiece. It was originally given by Lord Nelson to Sir William Hamilton, husband of the renowned Emma; one rather wonders why …

The east window illustrating the Ascension comes from the last century, presented by a local doctor who served as one of Nelson's surgeons at the Battle of Trafalgar. And there is a reminder of much more recent battles in the window commemorating casualties from the American

BELOW The beacon on the tower used to guide travellers when Weldon-in-the-Woods really was in the woods.

401st Bombardment Group, which was based nearby during the last war. It has a dove of peace taking off to replace the bombers flying through the clouds, and it also marks the friendships that grew up between the visitors and the villagers. Two hands are clasped between the Stars and Stripes and the Union Jack.

These references are easy to understand. In contrast, there is an abstract window installed only a few years ago, which is much more baffling. Different people interpret it in different ways, but its actual theme is the movement of the Spirit in creation through the seasons, and what looked to me like a pig in a pork-pie hat is really the globe, which is depicted in different corners of the window from Spring to Winter. Mixed in with them are Pentecostal tongues of fire, and the artist's idea of a mighty rushing wind.

The vicar, the Reverend Timothy Witherspoon, explained to me:

'The other windows are purely snapshots; some even have texts over them to give you the clue. But this one makes people think – of God in time, of Creation, of how the Spirit is alive today as it always has been. Does it fit in with the atmosphere of an old church? I think it fits in with the atmosphere of our age …'

RIGHT The abstract window represents the movement of the Spirit through the season, but different people have different interpretations.

IN MEMORIAM
JOHN
MASON
1904·
·1990

7 miles E of Nottingham on the A52

A statuette featuring a fish-seller – and a rood screen that featured Lily Langtry?

ST MARY'S HAS HAD MIXED FORTUNES with its rectors over the years. For half of the eighteenth century the office was held by the Revd Henry Stanhope, who for most of that period was 'incapable of duty by means of a phrensy'. His successor for the next fifty-odd years, the Rev. John Walker, was rather too energetic, spending most of his time devising new ways of extracting tithes from his parishioners. But while his only building project was a new rectory and a tithe barn for his own use, a later rector, the Revd Robert Miles, spent his money employing Sir George Gilbert Scott to restore the church and build the church school.

His wife and family were artists, and did much painting in the church, including the rood screen. It is said that his son Frank included on it the figure of Lily Langtry, the renowned Court beauty, whose portrait he had painted. Unfortunately the paintings were removed to make room for the 1914–18 War memorial, but Frank also designed his parents' memorial window, depicting Jacob's Ladder, and Jacob is thought to be his father as a young man, while other family members are angels.

The Revd Henry Hutt employed another notable architect, W. D. Caroe, to restore the church again from 1912 onwards, and among the furnishings he designed is the elaborate gilded reredos behind the altar, with its assortment of saints and townsfolk. In the fifties a very different designer, 'Mouseman' Thompson, made the altar rails bearing his 'signature' of a carved mouse. And finally, under the Rev. David Swain, the remarkable hanging cross was erected in 1992 as a World War Two memorial – nearly fifty years after the war. It is rich in symbolism, from the familiar Flanders poppy in the centre to the twelve silver balls which represent, rather unusually, the twelve apostles.

In contrast there is the uncomplicated and very lifelike statuette of Ann Harrison, a fish-seller who gave much of her income to St Mary's, and at the age of eighty-eight collected household scraps in her old fish-basket and sold them for pig food, to raise money for the Roll of Honour. Her friends had the statuette made after her death, aged 98, in 1928. Much more recently she has been commemorated in a way even further removed from that dominant hanging cross; a Bingham housing complex for elderly people has been named Harrison Court.

BELOW Ann Harrison, fish seller and devoted church supporter.

5 miles SE of Mansfield off the A617

A baby rocked in a cradle by the altar and Mary rocks an extra one in her arms

THE CONTRAST IN THE SETTING OF Blidworth church, as seen from the front and the rear, is quite remarkable. In front is a busy main road in a built-up area, hazardous both for parking and pedestrians. At the rear the church looks out from its hilltop, across the churchyard descending the hill below it, to the open country which used to be Sherwood Forest. The front, in fact, is modern, unromantic Blidworth; the rear is the Blidworth where Maid Marian lived, and where Will Scarlett, one of Robin's 'Merrie Men', is buried.

St Mary's has a rhyming reminder of the days when Sherwood Forest looked more like a forest. In the church is a memorial to Thomas Leake, a forest ranger, who was killed in single combat while on duty in the forest in the late sixteenth century. The lengthy inscription begins:

> *Here rests Thomas Leake,*
> *whose virtues were so known*
> *In all these parts, that this engraved stone*
> *Needs naught relate but his untimely end …*

And it ends, rather bitterly: '… he wasted in this wood, much of his wealth, and last of all, his blood.'

For many years the spot where he fell was marked by a massive stone. It was brought into the churchyard in 1836, but visitors are most likely to be attracted to the stone-built model of the church, some four feet high, which forms the centrepiece of the upper churchyard.

The Rocking Ceremony at St Mary's takes place on the Sunday nearest to Candelmas Day, when Mary was purified after the 'uncleanliness' of birth. The baby boy who is born in Blidworth nearest to Christmas Day is presented to the Holy Table and rocked in a Victorian cradle bedecked with flowers. In medieval times he was then carried in procession through the streets; one look at the road outside explains why this is not attempted today.

The church has two unusual illustrations of the Madonna and Child. One is on the pulpit, which came from Southwell Minster. Its plasterwork forms over thirty tiny heads, among them Mary and her baby. In a much more striking representation, a stained-glass window shows her cradling in her arms not one baby, but two. The first is Jesus, as shown in more orthodox portrayals; the other is a black baby.

BELOW The accurate model of the church provides an unusual centrepiece for the upper churchyard.
RIGHT The Madonna holds two babies; one is Jesus, the other is black.

Nan retired to her room over the porch – until there was no one at Holme

It must have been said many times before, especially by the people who live there, if only because of its inaccessibility: there is no place like Holme. On a small-scale map it is just off the A1 Great North Road, but between the A1 and Holme is the River Trent – and no bridge.

You have to drive south almost into Newark, then north again and down a dead end – but St Giles's is worth the effort. In an area rich in early medieval churches, this is one of the few Tudor ones, and it has remained almost unchanged, inside and out. It is a stocky, sturdy building with a stocky, sturdy tower surmounted by a stocky, sturdy broach spire, but its stockiest, sturdiest feature is the porch, with a priest's room on top, and a tale to tell.

St Giles's was rebuilt in its present form by a prosperous sixteenth-century wool merchant, John Barton. He was grateful for

the source of his wealth; it is said he inscribed on a window at his house: 'I thanke God and ever shall. It is the shepe that hath payed for it all.'

He is remembered by a more orthodox memorial window in the church, with some fine medieval glass, and he and his wife Isabella share a prominent and rather macabre tomb. Their effigies lie on top of it, and beneath is a third effigy, of a rotting corpse. But even this is not as macabre as the tale of the priest's room over the porch, or as it is known in local legend, Nan's Chamber.

Nan Scott lived in the village in 1666 when it was stricken by the Great Plague, and she took refuge in this room with a stockpile of food. From the window she could see the funeral processions of all her friends passing beneath her into the church as the village was gradually wiped out. When her food was exhausted she ventured out, and was appalled by what she found. She returned to her chamber until her death.

Visiting Nan's Chamber even today, three centuries later, the story is not difficult to believe. In it is a truckle bed made from an old chest, and a venerable Bible, and the blankets look nearly as old as the chest. Holme has long since returned to normal, but it is still a tiny, isolated community, and it was perhaps not surprising if Nan thought she was the only person left alive, not just in Holme but in the outside world as well.

RIGHT AND LEFT Interior and exterior of the priest's room above the porch where Nan Scott lived and died during the Great Plague.

8 miles SE of Oxford off A423

The bishop died of snakebite, but his flock were saved by the bell

THE LITTLE VILLAGE OF DORCHESTER may not be as well known today as its namesake in Dorset, but in Saxon times it was the centre of a diocese which spread as far north as the Northumbrian border. The first bishop was St Birinus, a missionary from Milan who converted the King of Wessex and carried on from there. There is no trace now of his cathedral, but the Normans built an Augustinian priory on the site, and in their church they had a shrine to St Birinus. The church has survived and it still has the shrine, handsomely restored in the 1960s.

The experts will probably direct you first to the church's splendid Jesse window, depicting Jesus' family tree in carved stonework and stained glass. Then there is the elegantly decorated Norman lead font, and the fourteenth-century sedilia with its traceried canopies. But the sedilia will bring you back to St Birinus, because his life is illustrated in its stained glass, and his story is rather more unusual than the window or the font.

Saints usually die a martyr's death, but it was a snake that killed Birinus. They were apparently rife in the Thames valley, and Birinus, as he lay dying, devised a way of saving his flock from a similar fate – and keeping them within reach of his monks at the same time. They would be immune from snakebite, he said, if they stayed within sound of the church bells.

There is no record in succeeding years of whether or not it worked, but it seems that the story of the bells' mystical powers as a snake repellent still, as it were, rang a bell. When a new tenor bell was presented to the church in 1380 the donor, a Mr Ralph Retwold, made a point of dedicating it to St Birinus, and since then it has been regarded as the bell which keeps the snakes at bay.

Sceptics will no doubt mock, but there is no denying that death by snakebite has been virtually eliminated within bell-range of Dorchester.

BELOW One of the church's oldest treasures, a thirteenth-century effigy of a knight drawing his sword.

5 miles SE of Abingdon off the A415

The tiny crusader that never was
– de Clare had nothing to declare

LONG WITTENHAM CHURCH HAS A VERY short Crusader. He is just two feet long, and he lies, not on a tomb, but on the edge of a piscina, the stone basin for pouring away water after Communion. Indeed he looks in imminent danger of rolling into it.

The effigy lies cross-legged, which usually indicates that the Crusader it commemorates served with distinction in the Holy Land. And experts say that small effigies were often installed when the deceased died abroad, and just his heart was brought home for burial. So it all suggests that the man it probably depicts, Gilbert de Clare, thirteenth-century Lord of the Manor who is known to have 'taken the cross', died in battle during the Crusades.

Alas, it was recently discovered that although he took the oath of a Crusader, he never actually went, and his heart is buried with the rest of him in Tewkesbury Abbey. One wonders therefore if his wife installed the effigy just to impress their descendants. Certainly no record has been found of any gallant deed by her spouse; de Clare, in fact, had nothing to declare.

However, Long Wittenham has another hero to fall back on. St Mary's has a copy of a sixteenth-century 'Book of Martyres' which refers to a John French of Longwitan, who was martyred in 1530 because 'he beleeved not the body of Christ, flesh, blood and bone, to bee in the Sacrament'. It does not state what happened to him, but

doubtless it was very nasty. His name is commemorated on one of the old houses in the village.

St Mary's had an unsung hero too, an unidentified churchwarden who shrewdly disguised the ancient lead font during the Civil War so Cromwell's men would not melt it down for bullets. He surrounded it with a wooden case filled with rubbish – and concealed it so successfully that it was not rediscovered for a couple of hundred years. Which is why it bears the inscription: 'Restored AD 1839, J. C. Clutterbuck, Vicar.' Mr Clutter buck made sure that at least *his* name would be remembered by posterity.

RIGHT Wittenham may be Long, but the effigy of one of its favourite sons is very short indeed. It fits on to the piscina.

1 mile NW of Wallingford off the A4130

They really did raise the roof to rebuild the church beneath it. But how?

ON SEPTEMBER 29 1884 THE *Abingdon Herald* published one of the great throw-away lines of local newspaper reporting. On the rebuilding of St James's church it said: 'The whole roof … was preserved intact, being simply raised six feet from its original height by leverage.'

Simply? By leverage?

The church guidebook registers understandable admiration: 'Surely a tribute to Victorian ingenuity and engineering,' it comments, but enquires no further. Yet this roof is made of solid oak, forty-eight feet long with a span of sixteen feet. Goodness knows how much it all weighs. So how on earth was it 'levered' off? And having been lifted six feet, how was it suspended in mid-air for what must have been several days, while the crumbling old walls beneath it were demolished and replaced? Not least, how did the workmen feel about having that great mass of wood dangling over their heads?

The questions must occur to anyone visiting St James's and reading its history. The answers must lie in the files of the diocese, or the architect, or the builder, if they still exist. Or in the memories of local families – it is only a couple generations back, and some eyewitnesses were still alive in the 1950s, like Mrs Brooker, the verger of the original church, who lived until she was ninety. Perhaps this gentle nudge will reveal the secret of how Sotwell literally raised the roof.

Meanwhile the roof is there to be admired, still held by two of its three original tie-beams; it helps the church to look much older than it is. One or two original windows were retained and a few bits of masonry from the old church have been incorporated, but they are difficult to spot. For instance there are two twelfth-century carved faces, 'high up on the north and south walls below the pseudo-corbels', but if you don't know a pseudo-corbel from a fake-sedilia, that doesn't help. The corbels are where the third tie-beam used to be, and

RIGHT The roof they literally raised to build new walls, forty-eight feet long with a span of sixteen feet.

on the north side you have to count down nineteen rows of stonework to find the rather jolly little face.

But they don't like to make things too easy in Sotwell, so I will let you find the other one yourself …

RIGHT AND BELOW A twelfth-century face is concealed among the nineteenth-century stones in the north wall. The one opposite is even more difficult to spot.

3 miles NW of Ludlow on the A49

The chancel that became a dining-room – then cherubs took over the ceiling

ST MARY'S IS PERHAPS THE ONLY PARISH church in England with a chancel which was once used as a dining-room in a private house, with a bedroom above. That curious episode in its history has been rather put in the shade by the quite astonishing ceiling which it now boasts, but a little blocked window in the east wall is a reminder of its secular period.

It happened after Henry VIII dissolved the priory which was founded there by twelve secular canons, who were granted a charter by Edward the Confessor 'to safeguard them from any interference, episcopal or otherwise'. It cut little ice with Henry. The buildings were acquired by a Charles Foxe, who used the materials to build a house on the site, incorporating the chancel as his dining-room. Two hundred years later the house was burnt down, all except – miraculously? – the dining-room. It was re-attached to the church; then came the painted ceiling.

Art critics are divided about this cheerful hotch-potch of billowing clouds, scantily-clad cherubs and festoons of texts. One describes it as 'a splendid piece of ecclesiastical pop-art'. Another likes 'its robust naivety'. A third says grudgingly: 'Not a great work of art, but no doubt the best that could be done at the time.' But as the artist was only paid seven pounds – hardly the cost of the paint and brushes – perhaps we should not be too demanding. Anyway, I think those twelve secular canons would have rather enjoyed it.

RIGHT A flavour of the decorated ceiling – 'a splendid piece of ecclesiastical art'?

St Mary's has memorials to two notable figures. There is a tablet in memory of Henry Hickman, an early nineteenth-century doctor who died when he was only thirty, too soon perhaps for his achievements to be recognized at the time. The tablet was only placed there a century later, to commemorate 'the first known pioneer in anaesthetics by inhalation'. The other memorial is the lychgate in memory of Augustus Selwyn, New Zealand's first bishop; his son was vicar of Bromfield for forty years.

Incidentally, the practice of adapting priory buildings for private use, instituted by Charles Foxe, still thrives in the twentieth century. The priory gateway has been converted into a holiday cottage.

1 mile W of Tenbury Wells off the A456

The triptych is full of Cornewalls – but their heart tomb has lost its heart

IN THE DAYS BEFORE REFRIGERATED VANS, undertakers had a major problem if an illustrious client died overseas – particularly if it was somewhere hot. Members of aristocratic families liked to be buried in the family chapel or vault, but transporting bodies for long distances in high temperatures was just not on. So the bodies were buried on the spot, but the hearts were often brought home to be interred, inside a lead box.

This is what happened to Edmund Cornewall, son and heir of the Baron of Burford, when he died at Cologne in 1436 during a tour of foreign parts. His servant buried him and brought home his heart, and it was placed in a 'heart tomb' on the chancel wall of St Mary's. The Cornewalls restored the tomb two centuries later, but about 1819 Edmund's heart unaccountably disappeared from it. Why anyone should want a 400-year-old human heart is not clear – unless the thief was more interested in the lead box which contained it.

Fortunately St Mary's is still rich in Cornewall monuments, the most prominent being right in the middle of the chancel, where it must cause congestion at weddings and funerals. A life-size wooden effigy of a later Edmund, who died in 1508, lies on top of a coffin-like chest. The figure is in armour and its head rests on a helmet, but Edmund was only twenty when he died and if he did ever wear them in battle, it could not have been for long.

RIGHT The heartless heart tomb of Edmund Cornewall; it was stolen early in the last century.

The most unorthodox Cornewall monument in St Mary's is a 1588 triptych, eleven feet high, on the sanctuary wall. The two doors are painted on the outside with the figures of twelve saints, but they open to reveal, not a biblical scene, but Richard Cornewall, ninth Baron of Burford, and his wife and eldest son, yet another Edmund. Behind the two small doors below is Edmund again, in his death shroud.

Next to the triptych stands another reminder of the Cornewalls, of a rather different kind. It is a fibreglass replica – the original was moved to the Tower of London – of a pole-axe, a massive medieval weapon of war. The initials on it are – inevitably – E. C. Yes, it has to be one of those Edmunds again.

6 miles S of Oswestry off the A465

First you spot the 'space-rocket' – then you see the writing on the wall

IT SOUNDS VERY WELSH AND INDEED Wales is only a couple of miles away, but Llanyblodwel has been in Shropshire since the sixteenth century, and it looks a typically English village – except for its church. There is nothing quite like St Michael's anywhere else in the country.

Outside the most striking feature is the tower – or is it the spire, or both? The two run into each other with no perceptible join, and the effect is rather like a rocket on its launch-pad, waiting for lift-off. It is over a hundred feet high, free standing except for a Gothic brick arch linking it to the church.

St Michael's was originally Norman, but it is hard to imagine. There is still an old door, and part of a fourteenth-century tombstone in the porch, carved with a hare being chased by a bodiless greyhound (only its head survives), but the rest of the building has been transformed.

The man responsible was the Rev John Parker, rector from 1845 to 1860, who combined several other interests with his

pastoral duties – and had enough money to indulge them all. He was an amateur architect, artist and carver, and St Michael's bore the full brunt of his efforts – although he did redesign the village school as well in his spare moments. The church exterior is not too startling apart from his sky-rocket – perhaps appropriate for a 'sky-pilot' – but inside the effect is quite dazzling.

All the available wall-space is covered with painted decorations and biblical quotations, and there is a profusion of elaborate carvings – galleries, screen, organ-case, pulpit, bench pews. There are so many distractions it must be no mean feat for a preacher to hold anyone's attention. By comparison the white-painted ceiling is quite sparsely decorated with red and blue fronds, but if you allow your eye to drop below the rafters, you are back among the quotations again.

On the arch between the tower and the church there is one more: 'From Lightning and Tempest, from Earthquake and Fire, Good Lord deliver us.' So far He has, but John Parker should have included vandals too, because after his death St Michael's suffered extensive desecration. Happily, it was completely restored in 1960, and a final inscription might have been added in his memory: 'Rest in Peace.'

LEFT Some of the Revd John Parker's decorative work in St Nicholas'; patterns, quotations, carvings. The Normans who built it might be impressed.
RIGHT John Parker's 'sky-rocket', his combined tower and spire. It may be an appropriate design for a 'sky-pilot'.

3 miles N of Tamworth off the A513

Tales from the tombs: a baby found in an eagle's nest, and a lethal tennis ball

POSSESSING SOME OF THE FINEST monumental effigies in the country can be a mixed blessing. St Peter's found itself faced with a bill of £50,000 in the last decade when the tiled floor began to buckle and the priceless alabaster figures began to break up. Happily, the work has been completed, and the tombs of the Ardernes, the Stanleys and their descendants, who owned the Elford estate for six centuries, have been made safe, one hopes, for a few centuries more.

The oldest one portrays Sir Thomas Arderne, who fought alongside the Black Prince, then restored and rebuilt the church. He is shown holding hands with his wife Matilda, normally a symbol of devotion, but it may also mean, it is said, that he married a rich heiress – and presumably is determined not to let her go.

Their great-grandson, Sir John Stanley, completed the south aisle and the chantry chapel in which the monuments are concentrated. His own shows him resting his head on a helmet carrying the crest of the Lathams, another earlier branch of his family. The eagle and child on the crest are a discreet reminder of a family peccadillo. It is said Sir Thomas Latham had an illegitimate son, and he devised a way of adopting him without offending his wife, who was barren. He had the baby placed in an eagle's nest in the garden, and when he and his wife 'discovered' it, she thought it was a miracle and urged they should bring it up as their own. He generously agreed.

The monument to Sir John's grandson tells a more obvious story, and a more tragic

BELOW The church is decorated with the shields of the Lords of the Manor from Saxon times.

one. The lad is holding a tennis ball – not the modern variety but a hard one as used in real tennis. Apparently, it struck him on the head and killed him. As a result, the estate passed to his sister, and came down eventually to the Pagets, who bequeathed it to Birmingham Corporation in 1937. Their Hall has since been demolished.

St Peter's and its monuments, however, still survive. Much of the church was restored in the last century, but unlike most Victorian 'restorations' it was made to look as much like Sir Thomas Arderne's fifteenth-century original as possible. In fact, with the monuments restored too, Sir Thomas and his wife may now be holding hands for quite a different reason: they are shaking hands on seeing a job well done!

ABOVE 'The Stanley Boy' holds the tennis ball that caused his death. They were rather more solid in those days.

10 miles SE of Leamington Spa off the A41

Quite a climb up the nave to the altar
– 'but it adds to the uplift of the spirits'

THE MOST OBVIOUS FEATURE OF All Saints' is its slope. From the floor of the tower to the altar there are five steps up into the nave, then the nave slopes steadily upwards until it reaches a couple of steps at the approach to the chancel, then there are more steps in the chancel itself – a total rise of ten-and-a-half feet. But nobody seems to mind; in fact, quite the contrary. The guidebook says, rather charmingly: 'The rise of the floor by sloping and steps to the bright chancel adds to the uplift of the spirits …'

Although the base of the tower is lower than the rest of the church, the top of it is of course much higher, and some say that Oliver Cromwell climbed up it to watch the nearby Battle of Edgehill – then descended,

more swiftly, by sliding down a bell-rope. It has also been suggested that his men stabled their horses in the church. But if every claim of this kind is true, the horses must have spent so much time in churches that Cromwell's army fought most of its battles on foot. Certainly a sceptical guidebook dismisses the story as 'Anti-Parliamentarian propaganda'.

On the other hand, it is not quite so dismissive of the suggestion that they were responsible for the shot-holes in the chancel arch. At one time a wooden Crucifix would have been there, and there are still traces of a painted Royal coat of arms. 'The early reformers would have been quite willing to shoot the Crucifix down,' it says, 'as would the Roundheads to shoot down the Royal arms.' Alternatively, as occurred in some other churches, could it merely have been the churchwardens shooting at the jackdaws in the roof?

But one relic of those stormy days is beyond dispute. After the Civil War the Royalist vicar was ousted and replaced by a Puritan minister, who used the Directory for the Public Worshippe of God which replaced the Church of England prayerbook. After the Restoration the parish clerk, Thomas Basse, took a dislike to the new vicar and hid the Book of Public Worshippe under his bed, along with the parish regis-

LEFT AND RIGHT Examples of the wall paintings and the ornamental pillar in the church.
OPPOSITE The climb to the altar, a rise of over ten feet from the other end of the nave, which uplifts the spirits.

ters. He only gave them back on his deathbed.

Basse's tombstone is in the churchyard, and for many years the Book of Public Worshippe was on display in a glass case in the church. To avoid vandalism however – and this time Cromwell's men could hardly be blamed – it is now kept in a safe place elsewhere.

3 miles E of Leamington Spa off the A425

Was this the burial place of a king?
It's the best idea on Offa

OFFCHURCH MAY SEEM A LONG WAY from Offa's Dyke, but it is said to be linked with it in two ways. It lies on the Welsh Road, the ancient drove road along which the cattle from the Welsh hills were driven, across Offa's Dyke, to the great markets in London and the Home Counties. The other link, a more tenuous one, is through Offa himself, the King of Mercia who created the earthwork named after him to mark the boundary between his kingdom and the Welsh. St Gregory's, which dates back in its origins to Offa's reign, has pieces of a stone coffin which,

according to tradition, was the one which contained Offa's remains. It is said he was buried here in AD796: why else should the village be call 'Offa's church'?

However, the first feature of the church which struck me – quite literally – was the door. The main door in the porch has a smaller one set in it, only about five feet high, and when I turned the handle I foolishly expected it to operate the whole door – and stepped briskly through. It was of course only the smaller door that opened, and the resultant impact was quite spectacular.

I am sure the Knightley family were better acquainted with this hazard – or perhaps they were only five feet tall. They were associated with St Gregory's from Henry VIII's time, when he granted them the village, until the death of Jane, Countess of Aylesford, in 1911. She is commemorated by the oak panelling behind the altar – a nice thought, but it does obscure some of the

BELOW Could it be the remains of Offa's tomb? After all, this is 'Offa's Church'. OPPOSITE An angelic judge or a child prodigy? The cherub in the wig is still a puzzle.

finer features of the medieval church.

However, St Gregory's has two mementoes of the seventeenth century which can still be clearly seen. There are pockmarks in the tower which are said to have been caused – like so many others – by the bullets of Cromwell's soldiers. And inside the church there is a memorial tablet which features, as well as the standard skull, a chubby-cheeked cherub wearing a very incongruous judge's wig.

The church guidebook admits to being baffled. 'The purpose of this macabre object is nowhere recorded.' So I can feel free to speculate. Either the deceased was a judge with an angelic disposition, or a child prodigy who passed his Bar exams while still in primary school.

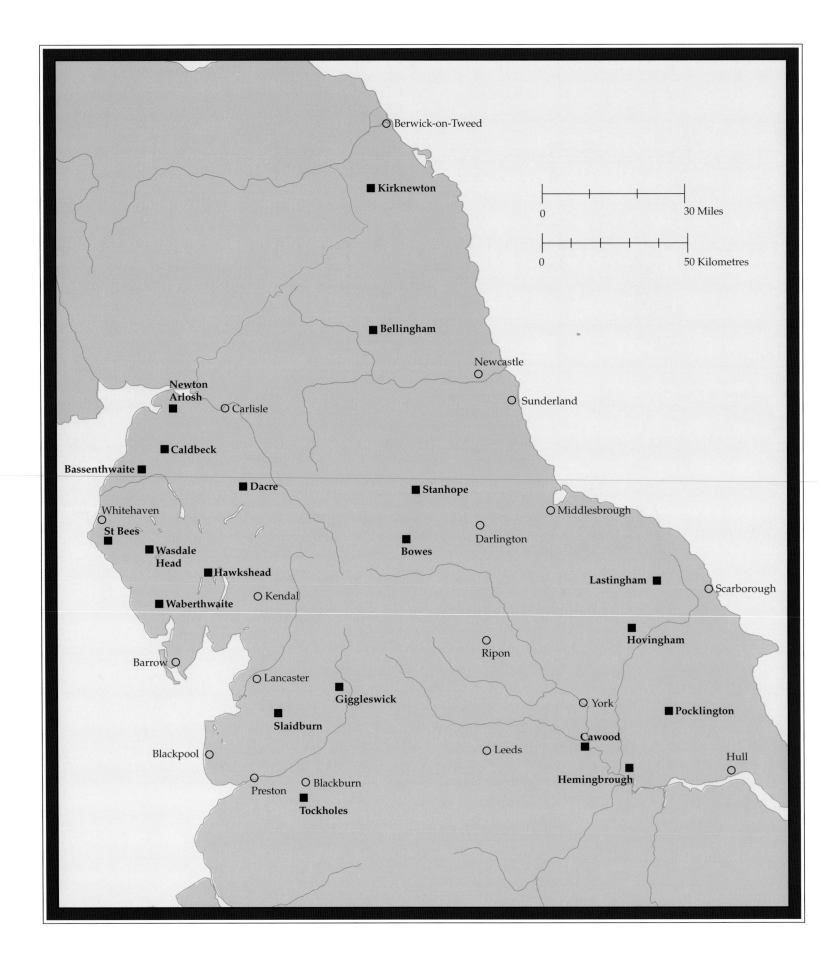

Berwick-on-Tweed

■ **Kirknewton**

■ **Bellingham**

Newcastle

Sunderland

Newton Arlosh ■

Carlisle

■ **Caldbeck**

Bassenthwaite ■

■ **Dacre**

■ **Stanhope**

Middlesbrough

Whitehaven

Darlington

St Bees ■

■ **Bowes**

■ **Wasdale Head**

■ **Hawkshead**

Lastingham ■

Scarborough

■ **Waberthwaite**

Kendal

Barrow

■ **Hovingham**

Ripon

Lancaster

■ **Gigglewick**

York

■ **Pocklington**

■ **Slaidburn**

Cawood ■

Blackpool

Leeds

Hull

Preston

Blackburn

Hemingbrough

■ **Tockholes**

0 ————————————— 30 Miles

0 ————————————— 50 Kilometres

4

NORTHERN ENGLAND

MANY ANCIENT CHURCHES IN NORTHERN England within range of the Scottish border were built like fortresses. One has a low, almost window-less chancel like a wartime bunker, another has a solid stone roof (perhaps to keep off flying haggises?), a third has an extremely narrow main doorway to make life difficult for marauding Scots. It also does not help funeral directors, bridal processions, or very broad worshippers. But northern churches can claim some of the finest settings in England, like the 'Climbers' Church' at Wasdale Head, beneath Sca Fell Peaks. It might also claim the lowest-beamed church roof; I mentally re-christened it, wincing, 'Wasdale-Mind-Your-Head' …

12 miles NW of Penrith off the B5305

'The sound of his horn woke me from my bed' – and services were abandoned too

IT COULD BE CONFUSING TO FIND THAT St Kentigern's church is close by St Mungo's Well. The two did not work as a team: they were the same person. St Kentigern, Bishop of Glasgow, came to Cumbria in the sixth century, and Caldbeck was one of the places, it is said, where he preached and baptized. He was so popular his friends called him Mungo, meaning 'well-loved'; but when they named the church's patron saint they kept to the more formal St Kentigern, and this is the name on his stained-glass window. The little figure of a friar in a bottom corner is not his alter ego, St Mungo; it is the 'signature' of the glaziers, who came from Whitefriars.

The Caldbeck name which most people would recognize best is neither Mungo nor Kentigern. This is Blencathra hunting country, and even if you have never heard of the Blencathra Pack, do y'ken John Peel, who founded it? Peel was born and died in Caldbeck and his gravestone is in the churchyard – it's the one with the hunting horn. He exchanged his marriage vows at St Kentigern, but only after he had run away to Gretna Green with his bride for the actual marriage. They were only twenty and eighteen, but it worked out happily.

Peel's devotion to hunting was contagious. At the sound of his horn, people not only 'woke from their bed', they rushed off to join him; even the parson, it is said, would abandon a wedding or a funeral. He hunted until a couple of weeks before his death, aged seventy-eight, and three thousand people came to St Kentigern's for his funeral. This time the parson was not tempted away …

Also in the churchyard is Mary Harrison, Wordsworth's 'Beauty of Buttermere', who was seduced by a bogus colonel, actually a bigamist and forger. He was caught and hanged, and Mary returned home to comparative obscurity, until a Caldbeck farmer, Richard Harrison, came to Buttermere to buy sheep, and took Mary home too. They were married, had seven children, and died within a year of each other. The gravestone commemorates them both.

Nearby is the headstone of a man who apparently died twice. The stonemason got as far as 'who died' at the end of a line, and presumably went off to a very good lunch. When he got back he failed to check where he had left off, and carved 'who died' on the next line as well. 'Peel's 'view-holloa', we are told, 'would awaken the dead' – but in this case he might have to 'view-holloa' twice.

BELOW John Peel's gravestone, complete with the inevitable hunting horn. Three thousand people came to his funeral.

St Andrew's, Dacre

The riddle of God's acre at Dacre: why were those four bears put there by our forebears?

ONCE UPON A TIME THERE WERE four bears. One was asleep with its head on a pillar, another had a cat on its back, a third was hitting the cat with its paw, and the fourth was asleep again, with a big smile on its face. It seems a simple little story, but it has been fascinating the experts for centuries. The four bears are still in the four corners of St Andrew's churchyard, and still nobody knows why.

One academic has suggested they were connected with the chained bear and 'ragged staff' on the arms of the Earls of Warwick, and may commemorate a marriage with the local lord's family. It was also thought they might have been on top of Dacre Castle. But there is no sign of a chain, the pillar they lean on is nothing like a ragged staff, and Dacre Castle still stands, so why move them? The simplest explanation is that the bears were put there in medieval times to tell a story with a moral, of a good bear overcoming an evil cat. It just seems a very labour-intensive way of telling it.

Inside St Andrew's there are more puzzles. A Viking cross-shaft depicts an apparently naked couple holding hands, and then another couple, with the woman in a skirt. There are assorted animals in between. Some say it is Adam and Eve before and after the Fall, others link it with Abraham and Isaac. The Vikings probably had a different story in mind altogether.

An even earlier stone portrays a figure with a big round face and ringlets, and for a moment I thought this might be a Saxon Goldilocks looking for those bears, but the head is attached to a lion's body, and it also has, disconcertingly, a large drooping moustache. Sort that one out for yourself!

The Hasells have been the local squires for three centuries, and there are many monuments to them in St Andrew's. Perhaps the most striking is the most recent, a window dedicated in 1994 to the memory of Edward Hasell's elder daughter, Sylvia Mary. It was engraved by Lawrence Whistler, and shows a Cumbrian landscape very like the view through the window. It includes her family home in the village, her Fell ponies, and the church where she was christened, and married, and buried. The inscription is from *Paradise Lost*: 'What if Earth be but the shadow of Heaven, and things therein each to other like…'

RIGHT One of the mysterious bears. Did they come off Dacre Castle, or do they just illustrate a story with a moral?

6 miles SW of Ambleside on the B5285

It is Wordsworth they like to remember – but Thomas Cowperthwaite wrote poetry too

ST MICHAEL AND ALL ANGELS IS A distinguished church in its own right, but like so many places in Lakeland, the name of William Wordsworth overshadows it. For instance, the stone bench along the east wall, where parishioners sat after services to hear public notices, is quite a rare survival, but visitors are generally more interested to hear that Wordsworth sat there as a boy, talking to the old gentlemen who used it.

Thomas Cowperthwaite was one of them, and his memorial, now set above the bench, notes that 'his facetious disposition ... made him respected by a numerous Acquaintance'. His facetiousness took the form of doggerel verse about his contemporaries. It may not be in quite the same class as Wordsworth's, but it has its own charm. For instance:

Matthew Hodgson, our widow'd Surgeon
Of late has had a heartfelt urge on
To gain the hand of Fanny Irton;
That he'll succeed is more than certain.

And he was right. They got married, had several children, and are buried together in the churchyard.

But even in the churchyard the Wordsworth connection takes priority. The guidebook devotes three pages to 'Wordsworthian Allusions' to it, and also mentions the grave of Thomas Park, 'drowned in Esthwaite water by falling through the Ice'. It comments: 'I mention him here primarily because it was with him that Wordsworth first went fishing ...'

Among the monuments and memorials inside the church, he is still not forgotten. One tablet is in memory of Thomas Bowman, headmaster of Hawkshead Grammar School for over forty years – 'he taught Wordsworth for two years', the guidebook notes. But there is no obvious link with the unusual 'Burial in Woollen' certificate on show by the door. To boost the wool trade, an Act enforced the use of woollen shrouds – one of the more macabre ways, it has been suggested, that the Government 'fleeced' the public.

The church ingeniously saved money by making the seventh-century parish chest out of a discarded tie-beam from the roof. It was hollowed out and fitted with the customary three locks for the vicar and churchwardens to hold separate keys. It may have contained some of Thomas Cowperthwaite's facetious verses – but unfortunately there were no unpublished works by William Wordsworth.

BELOW The long bench is quite a rarity – and not just because Wordsworth sat on it.

St John's, Newton Arlosh

14 miles W of Carlisle on the B5307

Safe from any marauding scots, but a bit tricky for the bride and groom

THE MAIN DOOR INTO ST JOHN'S IS precisely thirty-one inches wide, and only a little over six feet high. There is room, in fact, for just one person to pass though it at a time – and if that person is tall, he has to duck. This can obviously cause problems on occasions like funerals and weddings. It cannot be easy to man-oeuvre a coffin through such a tiny door-way, and when the bride and groom emerge after their nuptials, they can do so only one after the other. It is said locally that whoever comes out first will wear the trousers – though this seems a little unfair to cour-teous bridegrooms.

There was of course a very good reason for such a small entrance. Cumbria was under constant threat from the Scots when St John's was built in the early fourteenth century, and it was as much a fortification as a church. The walls are enormously thick, with tiny slit windows, and even if maraud-ing Scots got inside, the defenders could retreat up the tower and pick them off one at a time as they climbed the narrow stairs, while raising the alarm with the bell on the

BELOW St John's was built like a fortress, with enormously thick walls, tiny slit windows and a particularly narrow door.

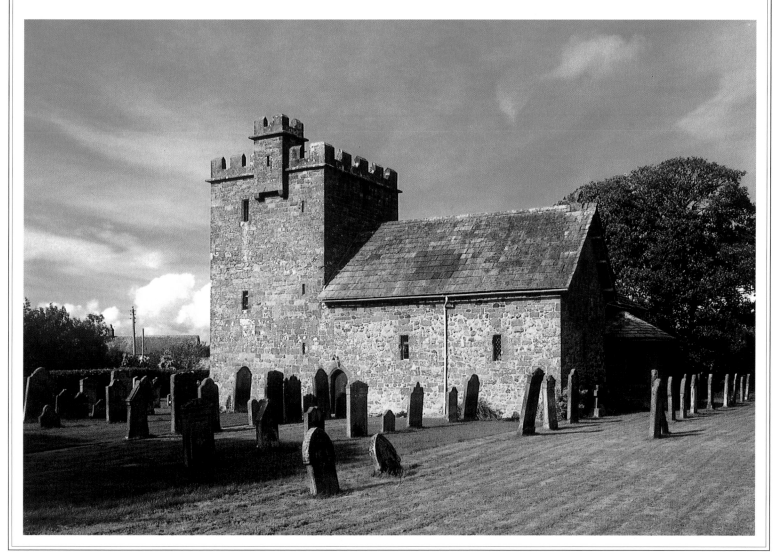

roof. In between raids the tower served as a lookout point, with panoramic views across the fields to the Solway Firth, and Scotland beyond.

What the Scots failed to achieve, however, was brought about by disuse and neglect after the Dissolution, and St John's was in a sorry state when the Victorians came to the rescue in 1843. They restored the little church and extended it sideways, moving the altar further along the new east wall. Most of this work was paid for by a philanthropic lady called Miss Sara Losh, who taught carving and sculpting; the two stone rams which flank the original site of the altar are her work. She also made the eagle lectern, giving the eagle an amused curve to its beak – and fifty years later it may have had something to smile about.

In another major restoration in 1894 the box pews were removed, and their replacements were installed at ninety degrees to the old ones, to face a new sanctuary in the north wall. This means that St John's is one of the few churches in the country where the congregation always sit facing northwards – and this perhaps is why the eagle is smiling, assuming it is a Scottish golden eagle. It must have realized that they are all permanently facing Scotland, as if on the watch for a belated raid across the border.

LEFT The main door is only thirty-one inches wide, causing problems for coffin-bearers and bridal couples.
OPPOSITE The eagle on the lectern seems to have an enigmatic smile. If it is a Scottish eagle one might guess why.

3 miles S of Whitehaven on the B5345; 18 miles NE of Whitehaven off the A66

She started in a snowstorm on the seashore and ended, like King Arthur, by the lake

WHEN THE IRISH ST BEGA landed at St Bees Head after escaping an enforced wedding to an amorous Viking, it is said she asked the local lord for some land to build a nunnery, and the lord – being a bit of a wag – said she could have all the land covered by snow on Midsummer's Day. He had not allowed for the Cumbrian weather; there was a heavy snowstorm on Midsummer's Eve, and Bega had all the land she needed.

Later the Normans built a priory there, and it is now the Church of St Mary and St Bega. It is still entered by their great west doorway, with its three sets of columns and elaborate decorations. St Bega is commemorated by a modern statue in her chapel, which shows her wearing her legendary bracelet. It was held in great veneration as a symbol of honesty; oaths were taken 'on the bracelet of St Bega'. Unfortunately someone stole it.

The church has an unusually macabre showpiece, a collection of relics from a coffin which was excavated in 1981. It contained one of the best–preserved medieval bodies in England, probably of a Crusader. The face, however, was distinctly gruesome; there is a startling photograph of it, together with the shroud in which the body was wrapped, still in excellent condition. There is also, oddly, a lock of a woman's hair found lying on his chest – his lover, perhaps? One day they may exhume another body – of a medieval bald lady …

St Bega herself moved away from the coast in her later years, and may well have settled and died in Bassenthwaite. There seems no other reason for the isolated location of St Bega's church, far away from any settlement when it was built in pre–Norman times. It has an unusual medieval lead crucifix and an Early English font, but it attracted little attention until the Lakeland poets discovered it, in the early nineteenth century. They were captivated by its romantic setting.

Wordsworth wrote about it, and Tennyson refers to it in *Morte d'Arthur*: 'The bold Sir Bedivere uplifted him … and bore him to a chapel in the fields, a broken chancel with a broken cross …' Edward Fitzgerald was there too, but failed to find similar inspiration. Instead, he won a contest amongst them for devising the weakest line in the fewest words. It was: 'A Mr Wilkinson, a clergyman".

BELOW The tiny St Bega's in Bassenthwaite
RIGHT Its imposing namesake at St Bees

16 miles S of Whitehaven off the A595

The pews now standing on platform one …
only joking, but this was where tomfoolery began

ST JOHN'S IS ONE OF THOSE SIMPLE little Cumbrian churches where little has changed over the years and you feel you are stepping back in time. In this case it is like stepping back on to a Victorian railway station, because the little box pews are still neatly numbered, like the compartments of a railway carriage. Pew No. 1 is perhaps the equivalent of first-class: it is at the back of the church, slightly raised for a better view, and extending right across the church, so it is large enough to house the small organ and – when available – a choir.

Pew No. 17 used to house the stubby Norman font, but as well as completely concealing it, the position must have been very inconvenient at baptisms. In 1973 a faculty was obtained to remove No. 17, and reveal the font – a block of sandstone which some say is the hollowed-out capital from a Roman pillar.

There are no other Roman remains around, but in the churchyard are the shafts of two preaching crosses which date back more than a thousand years. Until the last century they were built into the church porch, acting as a lintel and a doorstep. Nearby is another pillar which is actually a sundial, but it is so high it can only be read if you are very tall or happen to be riding through the churchyard on a horse.

Also in the churchyard is the grave of a seventeenth-century rector, William Grainger, 'one whom none called grasping', according to his epitaph. As the church guide points out, this rather suggests that rectors of that period quite often were. Perhaps the Latin inscription on the pulpit, which also dates from that time, hints at another of their failings: 'Woe is me if I preach not the truth.'

One of the bells at St John's is inscribed 'King Henry VI', and no one is quite sure why. But when Henry took refuge at Muncaster Castle, just across the river, after his defeat at the Battle of Towton, he left behind a drinking bowl in gratitude – and I suppose he might have had a spare church bell to leave behind as well …

The castle used to be reached from the church across a treacherous tidal ford, and it is said that two rectors have drowned in it – purposely misdirected by the castle steward, Thomas Skelton. Mr Skelton was a somewhat lethal practical joker whose name was the origin of the term 'tomfoolery'. I suspect that no one at St John's was terribly amused.

LEFT The pew doors are conveniently numbered, like compartments in old railway carriages. Presumably latecomers are often left with No. 13.

10 miles NE of Ravenglass on unclassified roads

Climbers now lie in the churchyard, but they once had to take the Corpse Trail

WASDALE HEAD IS ONE OF THE most remote corners of the Lake District, at the far end of Wastwater, which itself is the most rugged and inaccessible of its lakes, and certainly the deepest, reaching more than 250 feet in places. And St Olaf's, just thirty-three feet long, could be in contention as the smallest church in the country, but in fact fails to qualify because it was built as a chapel-at-ease, not a church. However, of all our churches or chapels-at-ease, it must surely be the lowest. It is the only one I know where you will bang your head on an overhead beam as you walk up the aisle, unless you remember to duck.

I think of it, in fact, not as Wasdale Head but as Wasdales Mind-Your-Head …

From the outside, St Olaf's is not the most glamorous of ecclesiastical buildings. It looks more like a long, low shed with a tiny belfry at one end. You have to stoop to look in through the windows. But inside it is a delightful, homely little church in miniature, and over the years it has been a haven for climbers, who have asked a blessing before they set out, and have given thanks on their safe return.

For some of them, though, it has been a last resting-place, as the inscriptions in its little churchyard testify. It lies beneath the massive Sca Fell Peaks and Great Gable, which can prove treacherous for the most experienced climber if the weather turns bad. Some of the tombstones mark the

graves of more than one climber lost in the same disaster; there are individual ones which record the death, for instance, of 'an only son killed on the central buttress of Scawfell'. One or two have been buried here, not because they died in an accident, but simply because they were, as one tombstone says, 'a climber in these hills', and wanted to return.

But in earlier days that would not have been possible. St Olaf's could not provide consecrated ground, and anyone who died in this valley had to be carried on the back of a packhorse to St Catherine's Church at Boot, on the far side of Burnmoor, along what used to be called the Corpse Trail.

Many tales are told of the precarious journeys made by the funeral parties, but one constantly recurs – of the packhorse that rebelled as it was hauled along the track, galloped off across the moor, still laden with its grim burden – and roams there still.

RIGHT Watch out for the low beam as you walk up the aisle. Wasdale Head might well be called Wasdale Mind-Your-Head …

4 miles SW of Barnard Castle off the A66

Dickens labelled him 'Wackford Squeers' – but he has a memorial window

PIECES OF ROMAN STONE INCORPorated in the walls of St Giles's, and a Roman dedication stone inside the church, date back to the time when Bowes was known by the unattractive name of Lavatrae – it probably just meant that washing facilities were provided there for the legionaries marching along the Stainmore Roman road. However, in Victorian times it acquired a reputation as unfortunate as its Roman name, when it was a main dropping-off point for boys despatched from the south to the institutional boarding schools, or 'boy farms', which proliferated in the area.

St Giles's has some reminders of that era too. In the churchyard are the graves of William Shaw and his family, and nineteen-year-old John Taylor. Shaw was the proprietor of one such school, and Taylor was one of his pupils. It is widely assumed that Charles Dickens based Dotheboys Hall in *Nicholas Nickleby* on Shaw's Academy, using Shaw as the model for Wackford Squeers, and Taylor as the hapless Smike. Certainly Dickens got the idea when he was staying at the Unicorn Inn at Bowes and watched boys coming off the long-distance coaches, looking understandably apprehensive. Shaw's Academy, after a period as a café and now converted into cottages, actually bears the name Dotheboys Hall.

It is a pity this shadow hangs over Bowes, because the village is pleasant enough and the church has other attributes besides its links with Dickens. It has fine Norman

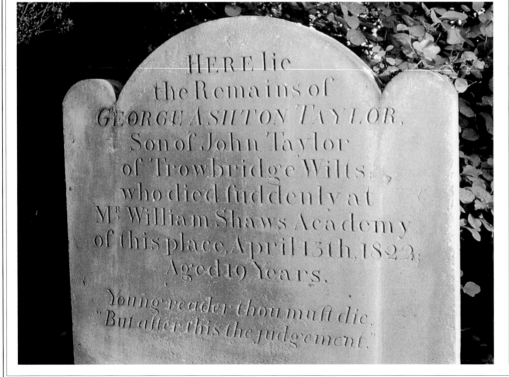

LEFT AND ABOVE Reminders of two characters associated with Dickens's Dotheboys Hall: George Taylor and William Shaw.

doorways and two ancient fonts, one Norman, the other a little later. However, the most talked-about feature of the building is probably a memorial window which was installed in 1895 – to William Shaw.

After the publication of *Nicholas Nickleby* the public reaction forced Shaw's Academy to close, and Shaw himself was ruined. But his family maintained that Dickens had painted far too black a picture. An enterprising lawyer might have persuaded them to sue for defamation – rather like one of his own novels – but instead, Shaw's granddaughter had the window placed in St Giles's, in an attempt to restore his good name. It seems to have been a forlorn hope.

St Thomas's, Stanhope

The church that lost its hump – and got fossils in the font

MOST COUNTRY CHURCHES HAVE changed their appearance over the centuries, and St Thomas's has done so rather strikingly, but it has changed its patronal saint as well. When it was built in the twelfth century it was dedicated to St Mary and St Thomas à Becket – the assassination of the Archbishop of Canterbury must have been very fresh in everyone's minds. At some stage, however, home-grown saints became unfashionable and St Thomas the Apostle took over.

The striking alteration to the building has been to its roof. Until the nineteenth century it was hump-backed: early prints make it look rather like a tortoise, with the tower sticking up instead of a neck. The Victorians obviously didn't fancy it, and replaced it with the standard roof it has today.

St Thomas's has its fair share of medieval panelling and stained glass, but its two most unusual relics have been imported from the moors above Stanhope. One is a Roman altar, dedicated to the forest god Sylvanus; according to the inscription it celebrated a successful hunt for wild boar. The other is older by about 250 million years, a fossilized tree-stump by the churchyard wall; it was dug out of a local quarry. But it is not the only fossil at St Thomas's: the font is made from local Frosterley marble, a limestone which contains fossil remains from the days when the sea was not too far away.

It was none of these curious items, however, which made Stanhope a very popular incumbency in the eighteenth century. It

ABOVE AND LEFT The fossilized stump still remains after 250 million years, but the church 'hump' was replaced by a more standard roof.

was due to a shrewd rector called Isaac Basire, who was appointed to the living while he was a chaplain to Charles I. Before he could take it up the Civil War broke out and he fled to France. He kept up his connections in high places, however, and when the monarchy was restored and he returned to take up his living, he somehow managed to get a Bill through Parliament which granted him and his successors a tenth of all the income from the lead-mines in Upper Weardale.

Stanhope became known as the 'golden living', the richest in the North of England. When it all changed and clergy received standard salaries, perhaps that was when the church roof lost its hump-back, and the rector got the hump instead …

7 miles N of Clitheroe on the B6478

Dog-whips in church to control the dogs – but the problem was also the people

ST ANDREW'S WAS COMPLETELY REBUILT in 1450, and it is difficult to spot the few reminders of what was there before – just the battered remains of two tombstones, one outside the east wall and the other in the north wall inside the church. The first is carved with a bow and some steps, the symbol of a thirteenth-century forester of the Forest of Bowland, in which Slaidburn lies. The other has what looks like the blade of a hatchet, emblem of another forest official.

One of the earliest fittings of the present building is the sanctuary bar, a wooden pole which could be slotted across the door if a fugitive claimed sanctuary, giving him at least a temporary respite. And in the vestry is another form of protection, a pair of dogwhips, from the days when the congregation brought their dogs into church. As well as fending off any that became too belligerent, the dog-warden used the whips to break up any fights between the dogs themselves. St Andrew's

had a dogwarden for over a hundred years, from 1760 to 1863, and each was paid between five and ten shillings a year, depending perhaps on how many fights he stopped – or how many times he got bitten …

There was a much earlier period, however, when brawls nearly broke out among the worshippers themselves, over who should sit in the Hamerton Chapel. The Hamertons were Lords of the Manor and benefactors of the church for centuries, but Sir Stephen Hamerton joined the protest against Henry VIII's dissolution of the monasteries and was hanged in 1537. His son and heir Henry died of grief in the same year, and his widow died a few months later.

The family forfeited most of its estate, and some of it went to a Cuthbert Musgrave, who insisted on sitting in the Hamerton Chapel. This was not at all popular with the locals, and one family called Battersby, who were long-term tenants of the Hamertons, barracked Musgrave during a service, calling him a thief and murderer. Musgrave went to law and got judgement against them but the feud continued for years.

Happily the chapel is much more peaceful now. After being out of use for some time, it is being restored to its original purpose as a place of prayer and regular worship, its altar a Jacobean chest which many generations of the Hamertons would remember.

LEFT The Hamerton Chapel was the scene of unseemly exchanges which led to a lawsuit. It is more peaceful now.

3 miles S of Blackburn off the A666

A wooden church replaced the old one, but the stone pulpit in the churchyard still survives

ST STEPHEN'S IS AN UNLIKELY LOOKING church for such an ancient churchyard, one of the most extensive in England, where places of worship have stood for longer than anyone can tell. As an old church guidebook elegantly put it: 'The date, agency or circumstances whereby the Christian message was first brought to and established in this hamlet lies in the unrecorded and forgotten past.' But the current church, built less than forty years ago, is a simple wooden building only thirteen feet high, with a prefabricated roof like a modern barn. It could hardly be in greater contrast to its predecessor, built in 1833 to seat nearly nine hundred people.

It was not only built big, it was built badly. After a long losing battle against various structural problems, it was decided in the 1960s to demolish it and erect a more practical, 'temporary' building – which actually is similar in size to the pre-1833 church. That was almost as low and only fifty feet long.

The special feature at St Stephen's is not in the building itself but in the churchyard: its very unusual outside pulpit. Fortunately it was not attached to the previous church, or it might have been demolished with it. Instead it was built on to the wall of the old school, which flanked the churchyard. During the incumbency of the Revd A. T. Corfield, at the turn of the century, annual outdoor services were held, conducted from a wooden pulpit which came from Mellor

church, where Mr Corfield's father-in-law was vicar. In 1910 he replaced it with a stone pulpit which he and two friends made from the fifteenth-century stonework of Gerstaine Hall, one of the many buildings demolished by Liverpool Corporation for a massive waterworks scheme.

Even when the old school was replaced, the services continued; just one classroom was preserved, the one to which the pulpit was attached. A newspaper cutting of 1921 reports how visitors from Blackburn and Darwen flocked to that year's service – even

though the trams were not running. 'Their uphill journey in the somewhat overpowering heat along the parched field paths and the dusty highway was however well recompensed ...'

Alas, the enthusiasm did not last, and the services were discontinued. Just occasionally, if congregations overflow into the churchyard, an auxiliary cleric presides from the old stone pulpit, but its only use in recent years was after an open-air flower festival. When the exhibits were sold, it made an excellent rostrum for the auctioneer.

RIGHT The stone pulpit was originally used for annual outdoor services. Now it sometimes serves as an auctioneer's rostrum.

12 miles N of Hexham off the B6320

Difficult times: chicken-bones in the piscina, cannon-balls in the roof …

NO DOUBT ABOUT IT, ST Cuthbert's has had a rough time over the centuries. The masons who built it in 1180 apparently knew what to expect, because instead of a standard wooden roof – far too easy to burn – they gave it one made of stone. When it was restored in the seventeenth century they merely added new stonework on top of the old. Later they had to add buttresses to the already massive walls to stop them bulging outwards with the weight of the roof. One sympathetic writer says of St Cuthbert's now: 'It has an air of fortitude …'

During the Border raids there was a fight around the church in which eleven men were killed. Three cannon-balls were found many years later, embedded in the roof; they are now in a glass case in the church. When the raids ended St Cuthbert's was in a sorry state: the building was almost a ruin, the font was broken, there was just one Communion service a year, and there were no books at all – perhaps because the clerk could not read or write.

The church was restored, but the violence continued. In 1710 a regular church-goer killed a man in a duel. He was pardoned, but perhaps as a macabre

BELOW Under the Long Pack tomb slab lies a robber who hid inside a pedlar's pack – and was shot when he twitched.

revenge, his opponent's body was buried just beside his pew. He never entered the church again.

The church had deteriorated again by 1843, when an inspector found green mould all over the walls, chicken bones dumped in the piscina, which should have held holy water, and human bones exposed under the gallery. The deal altar was converted into a cupboard with two doors 'which give it a strong resemblance to a kitchen dresser!'.

Happily, more restorations have taken place, the most recent in 1997, when ex-pupils of a local school returned for a reunion, found St Cuthbert's had problems again, and contributed thousands of pounds towards repairs. And through all these vicissitudes, St Cuthbert's Well, just outside the churchyard, has continued to flow. Its clear water, once credited with healing powers, is still used for baptisms and at the Eucharist.

The 'Long Pack' tomb slab in the churchyard survives too, with the story of a maid at a local mansion who allowed a peddler to leave his pack in her kitchen. She saw the pack move after he left, so another servant put a shot in it, and killed a robber concealed inside. He was never identified, and lies under the Long Pack slab.

Just another average incident in the stormy history of St Cuthbert's …

RIGHT St Cuthbert's exceptionally heavy stone roof, built to last.

10 miles W of Wooler on the B6351

Built like a bunker against the Scots – but three got in anyway

ST GREGORY'S SERVES ONE OF THE largest parishes in the country, covering more than forty thousand acres once occupied by fifteen medieval townships, but the size of the parish is hardly reflected in the size of the church. It could be in the running for another title: the low-est chancel in the country, with side walls only three feet high to support the barrel-vault roof. The south transept is even more claustrophobic, with no upright walls at all: the roof slopes inwards from the floor.

There was of course a reason for this when they were built in the fifteenth cen-tury. The church served as a defence post against the marauding Scots, only a dozen miles away across the border. The much more vulnerable nave and tower were built in the nineteenth century, when it was hoped the threat had passed.

The reason for the church's dedication to

LEFT St Gregory's was built like a defence post against the Scots, after they wrecked the previous one.

St Gregory the Great is a little obscure, but it does exist. It originates from the visit of Bishop Paulinus, a Roman monk who was sent to Kent by Pope Gregory in the seventh century. He came north with the King of Kent's daughter when she married the King of Northumbria, and spent a month at his palace at Gefrin, about a mile from the site of the present church. He converted the locals and baptized them in the nearby River Glen, and the church developed from that.

The original building was not nearly as bunker-like as its fifteenth-century successor, and when the Scots turned nasty there were several periods when it lay ruined and derelict. It was thought such an easy target that at one stage the bishop gave the vicar special permission to say Mass anywhere else in the parish he fancied.

ABOVE The bunker-like chancel could keep out marauders, but three Scots got in, disguised as the Magi!

Once the church was rebuilt the Scots never took it, but there does seem a distinct Scottish flavour about its greatest treasure, a relief of the Adoration of the Magi. Experts differ about its age; estimates range from the ninth to the twelfth centuries. But one feature of it seems beyond dispute. The Three Wise Men are wearing kilts …

4 miles NW of Selby on the B1223

It stands on little more than a modest mound, but it contains an immodest mountain

ALL SAINTS' IS BUILT ON THE HIGHEST point in the village – all of 29 feet 3 inches above sea level, according to the bench mark on the tower. From that position, on the bank of the Ouse, the original church had a grandstand view of the Vikings sailing up the river to pillage York, and the Normans doing much the same a little later. But nothing is left from that period; the earliest part of the present building dates back a mere eight centuries. By that time, Cawood Castle had become the established home of the archbishops of York, and All Saints' did quite nicely from this illustrious connection.

One indirect perk, according to local legend, is its tenor bell. When Edward I, Hammer of the Scots, went off to do some more hammering, he left his wife and Court with the archbishop, and when he returned with the spoils of war he presented him with this bell for his chapel, as a thank-you for his hospitality. It was also probably simpler than carting the great chunk of metal down to London. When the chapel was destroyed during the Civil War, the bell was transferred to All Saints'.

It was also during the Civil War, so it is thought, that the ancient stone altar slab was sunk into the floor of the vestry to prevent it being damaged by Cromwell's men. It stayed there for nearly three hundred years, until an observant incumbent spotted the five crosses on it, representing the wounds of Christ, and put it back in place in 1930.

All Saints' has two notable memorials, commemorating very different people from very different backgrounds, in very different ages: George Mountain and James Meggison. Mountain was a local man who became Bishop of Lincoln, then of London – and planned to be Archbishop of York. In 1628, when the king sought his advice on the appointment, the reply he gave was ingenious – and somewhat shameless. 'Hadst thou faith as a grain of mustard seed,' he said, 'thou wouldst say to this mountain' – and he indicated himself – 'be removed to that sea.' The king got the point – and Mountain got the See of York. It was perhaps poetic justice – or something more? – that he died only a fortnight after his enthronement.

He has a very grand monument, his bearded effigy surmounted by his coat of arms. James Meggison just has a small plaque on the stall where he sang as a choirboy. In 1930 he became a galley boy on a brand new airship for its maiden flight; it was the ill-fated R101…

LEFT George Mountain, briefly an archbishop.

1 mile W of Settle off the A65

The effigy lies on a horse's head 'pillow' – but a horse with a beard and horns?

ST ALKELDA, ACCORDING TO LEGEND, was a Saxon martyr strangled by a couple of Viking women, who could apparently be just as ruthless as their menfolk. So it is appropriate that her church should be fitted with an 'invasion beam', which is set into the thickness of the wall and can be drawn across the door into a socket on the other side, thus excluding any other potential stranglers.

Nonconformists, however, are welcome. There is a memorial tablet in the church to Richard Frankland, who famously told Charles II to his face: 'Reform your life, your family, your kingdom and the church!' He was twice excommunicated, but twice absolved. And on the opposite wall is a portrait of Dr George Birkbeck, the Quaker who founded the Mechanics' Institutes, forerunners of the Workers' Educational Association.

But it is the monuments to the Tempest family which have the strangest tales to tell. The effigies of Dame Sybil and Dame Mabel, wives of Sir Richard Tempest, were dug up during restoration work in the 1890s. Their heads were missing and the bodies were badly knocked about, but some of the colouring on their robes survived, the crimson and white of the Guild of Corpus Christi of York.

The effigy of Sir Richard himself lies elsewhere in the church, near the site of the Tempest Chancel. He had, as one might expect, a stormy career: he was knighted at the Battle of Wakefield in 1460, but charged with treason the following year, only to be pardoned by Edward IV. When he was buried in 1488, according to the church guide, the head of his charger was buried with him – and inde ed, other travel guides have said the same.

I have speculated in the past on how this bizarre interment could have taken place. It seems unlikely that he and his horse died simultaneously – unless they fell off a cliff together, or the old chap got involved in a fight. So had the horse already died, and its body was dug up for the head to be reburied? Or was the unfortunate animal slaughtered to accommodate Sir Richard's last request?

Happily, neither of these gruesome alternatives seems likely. Experts point out that the animal's head which acts as a pillow for Sir Richard, and which may have given rise to this story, does not belong to a horse but a goat, symbolizing the Tempest crest. And indeed one can still make out the horns and the beard. Horse-lovers may breathe again.

RIGHT Sir Richard Tempest uses an animal's head for a pillow – not a horse, it seems, but a goat.

5 miles E of Selby on the A63

An outsize spire, a jester in the pews, and the oldest bottom-rest in the business

St mary's was the last church in the North to which the collegiate system was applied, and although that distinction disappeared with Henry VIII, along with its provost, three prebendaries, six vicars and six clerks, its grandeur has survived. It is built as a cruciform with a central tower, surmounted by a quite astonishing spire, twice the height of the tower itself and rising to 180 feet above the ground – a landmark visible for many miles across the flat Plain of York.

It was the work of Prior Washington of Durham, who established the collegiate church and enlarged it accordingly. He put a row of carved washing tuns, or tubs, around the tower as a rather jolly pictorial signature. The tip of the spire was renewed in the 1980s, and a new weathervane was put in place by Karen Keating of 'Blue Peter', recorded by the television cameras – another kind of pictorial signature in an electronic age.

The craftsmen who carved the bench-ends in the nave had some fun too, epitomized by the jester on one of the pews, complete with cap and bells. Their assorted wild beasts, two-headed dragons and naked men in peculiar poses even spread to the medieval parish chest with its decorated

panels; but the showpiece among the carvings is a misericord dated about 1200 – making it probably the oldest carved bottom-rest in the country.

Incidentally, the tradition of grotesque carvings has continued into the twentieth century. A gargoyle on the roof, with pointed ears, a belligerent nose, saw-edged teeth and a sinister leer, was carved by a stonemason from Hull in 1994 – perhaps illustrating the ancient beggars' prayer, 'From Hull, Hell and Halifax, good Lord deliver us …'

Hemingbrough must have had its unattractive moments too. A memorial in the churchyard to Daniel Driscol of Tottenham records that this unsuspecting southerner was waylaid and murdered on a local common in 1868. But the village's reputation for honest citizenry is restored by another tombstone from the same period, in memory of Robert Cocker, who died aged eighty-six after working for the same farmer for fifty-five years 'with credit and esteem, duty his sole aim and principle'. This paragon was also 'a truly good neighbour void of offence, a kind husband and benevolent father, happy with the welfare of his family'. And according to the final summing-up, 'his life was ever an example of sobriety, of industry and fidelity – rarely equalled in this world.'

How true …

LEFT The misericord is dated about 1200, arguably the oldest in the country.
RIGHT The tower is decorated with washing tuns in honour of Brior Washington. Above it, the spire rises to 180 feet.

6 miles SE of Helmsley on the B1257

Worsley country and a Worsley church
– but the Saxons had a hand in it too

THIS IS VERY MUCH WORSLEY country. I remember, as a young reporter, meeting a little lad from Hovingham before the wedding of the Duke of Kent in York Minster, and I asked him if he knew who was getting married. 'It's our Miss Worsley,' he said – then added, as an afterthought, 'I don't know who t'man is …'

Similarly, All Saints' is very much a Worsley church. The family have been Lords of the Manor and benefactors of the church for many generations. One of them virtually rebuilt the place in 1860, and it is filled with Worsley memorials. But mercifully the ancient Saxon tower was left unscathed, and All Saints' still has some great treasures from its pre-Conquest days.

The oldest is the stone carved with a cross which is set in the masonry over the door; its design indicates that it is some twelve hundred years old. It was probably part of the original church, no doubt destroyed by Viking invaders. The Saxons who rebuilt it must have salvaged the stone from the rubble and installed it over the door. They also placed a tenth-century 'wheel cross' high up on the tower.

But the church's most striking relic is the great Viking Cross in the chancel, which probably stood in the open to mark the site of Christian worship after the earliest church was demolished. The Saxons incorporated the cross into the masonry of the tower, along with their other salvaged treasures, and it stayed there for nine centuries. Then in 1925 it was brought inside and mounted on the wall of the south chapel – 'as a kind of museum piece', says the church guide. When the chancel was re-ordered in 1981 – by the Worsleys, naturally – the cross was mounted on a modern wrought-iron pedestal and now acts as a unique altar cross.

The other great treasure of All Saints' was also extracted from the wall of the tower – which must have displayed an impressive mosaic of the early masons' craft when all these pieces were in place. It is the Saxon stone which now serves as the reredos in the Lady Chapel carved with eight figures in high relief. The outer ones are angels, but those in between have been weathered beyond recognition. As that little lad might have said: 'I don't know who t'men are.' But wouldn't it be nice if they were very early Worsleys?

BELOW The Saxon stone in the Lady Chapel may well have been the lintel over the original church door.

St Mary's, Lastingham

8 miles NW of Pickering off the A170

Down the steps, through the doors – and back a thousand years

IN ANY OTHER BUILDING THE FLIGHT OF steps descending from the middle of the nave in St Mary's might well lead to a cloakroom, but here they lead to the great treasure of Lastingham, the Norman crypt marking the burial place of the Saxon bishop Cedd, founder of a monastery on this site in AD654. The area was populated mainly by wild beasts and robbers, and the monks who accompanied him might well have pleaded: 'Enough, Cedd!' But they completed the monastery, and Cedd was abbot for ten years before dying, not violently, but from the plague.

His brother Chad took over, and built a church in which his remains were interred. After the Conquest, some of the stones and perhaps the altar were used by the Abbot of Whitby to build the crypt as a shrine to Cedd's memory, and he half-built an abbey church above it when he was moved to York. It was never completed, but it has been large enough as a parish church ever since.

BELOW The Norman crypt is a shrine to St Cedd, the Saxon bishop who established a monastery here.

St Mary's itself has some unusual features, like the Calvary which came from a Spanish warship captured at the Battle of Cape St Vincent, but it is the crypt which attracts all the attention. One guidebook quotes the line, 'Brothers, we are treading where the saints have trod', and that indeed is how it feels as you pass through its doors and step back a thousand years.

But life at St Mary's has not always been untroubled. Eighteenth-century vicars were inclined to live elsewhere and leave the parish work to underpaid curates. One of these, the Revd Jeremiah Carter, had thirteen children, and to supplement the family income his wife kept the Blacksmith's Arms just across the road, and he sometimes played the fiddle there to entertain the customers after church. When the archdeacon queried this extramural activity, Jeremiah penned this admirable reply:

'My parishioners enjoy a triple advantage, being instructed, fed and amused all at the same time. Moreover, this method of spending their Sunday is so congenial with their inclinations, that they are imperceptibly led along the paths of piety and morality.'

I think Cedd would have approved, and so would Chad. Like his much later namesake, he might have observed: 'Wot, no applause!?'

LEFT The steps in the central aisle lead down to St Cedd's crypt. Sidesmen must have got used to avoiding them as they take the collection.

220

12 miles E of York off the A1079

A buried cross, A lovesick prioress, and a 'Flying Man' who crashed on the roof

ALL SAINTS' IS SO RICH IN UNEXPECTED stories it is difficult to know where to start, but the earliest must relate to the fourteenth-century stone cross in memory of John Sotheby which now stands near the font. It was found buried in the churchyard in 1835. Presumably it was hidden there during the Civil War, and nobody bothered to dig it up again. It is now one of the church's greatest treasures.

Then there is the 'treasure tomb' by the chancel of Gyles Bateson, in which thieves once hid their loot behind a loose panel, and below the pulpit is the 1512 gravestone of Margaret Easingwold, with a Latin inscription describing her as 'Prioress of this place'. According to legend she and the local parson, John Dowman, were in love, but being in Holy Orders he could not marry her, so she went off to a nunnery and he busied himself founding Pocklington Grammar School.

When she died and was buried in the nunnery her spirit was so restless, it is said, that the nuns brought her back to All Saints', along with her gravestone, to be buried close to her former love. Near the stone's original position in a side aisle another slab was uncovered, bearing the initials 'J.D.' The school has been linked with the church ever since – though less romantically – and there is a special pew for the headmaster and his usher.

However, the memorial with the strangest tale is outside the church on the chancel wall, a much-worn plaque recording the death in 1733 of Thomas Pelling, 'A Flying Man'. He was killed, according to the burial register, 'by jumping against the battlement of ye Choir when coming down ye rope from ye steeple'. Mr Pelling, it seems, was a travelling stuntman who donned batlike wings attached to his arms and legs, and suspended himself by one heel from a pulley on a rope. The rope was attached to a pinnacle on the tower, and the other end should have been held taut by a windlass near the former Star Inn, but it was allowed to slacken and the Flying Man crashed into the roof.

More happily, there is the 'memorial' carving in the north aisle depicting two men wrestling. It is said a mason told his son he was too young to be a carver, so when the church was empty the lad did this carving, showing him wrestling with his father, to prove his skill. On the other hand, it could just be Jacob wrestling with the Angel.

RIGHT John Sotheby's cross, found buried in the churchyard after 500 years.

INDEX

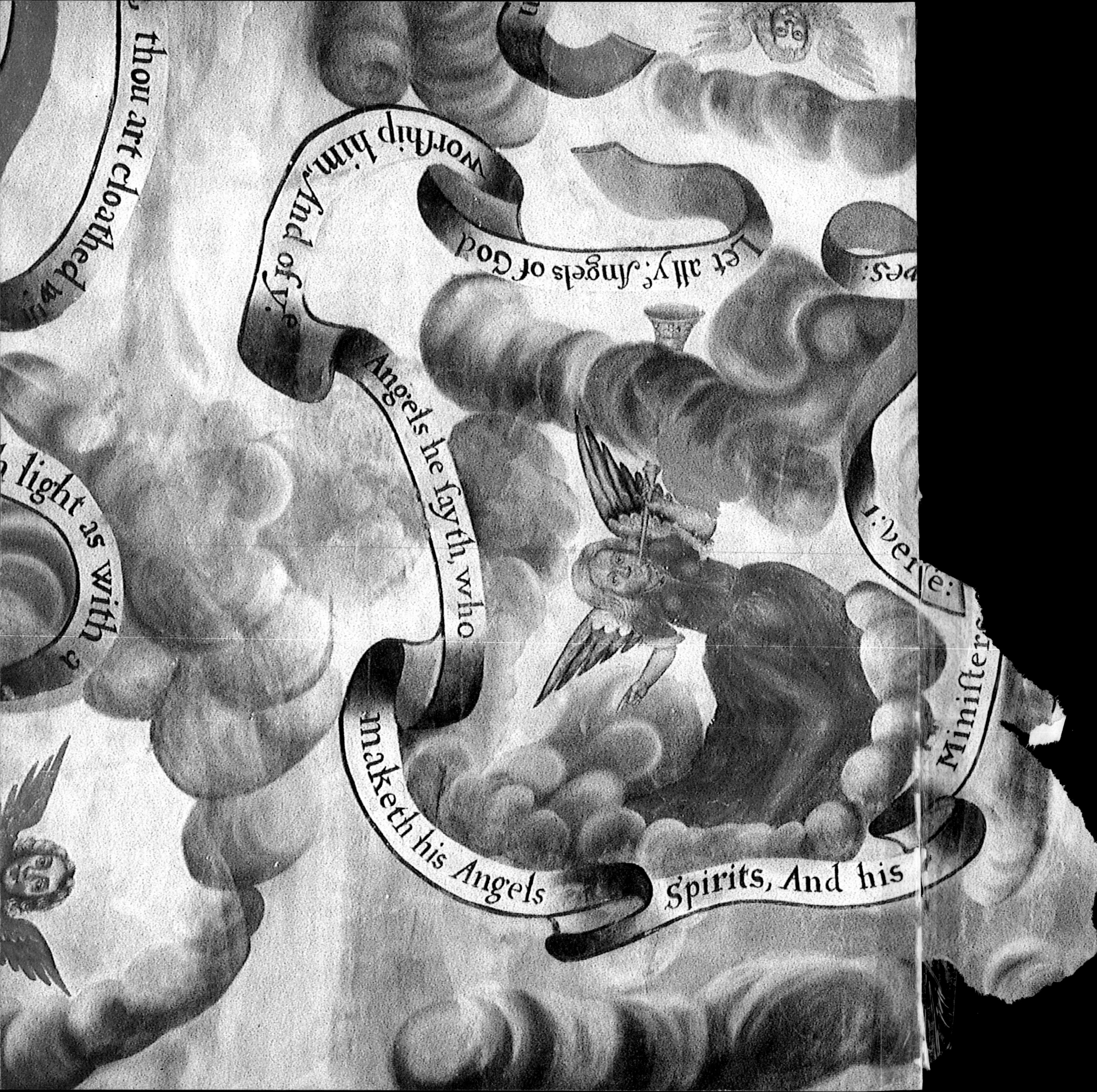

thou art cloathed wi...

Worship him, And of ye

Let all ye Angels of God

Angels he fayth, who

light as with a

maketh his Angels

Spirits, And his

Ministers

veríe:

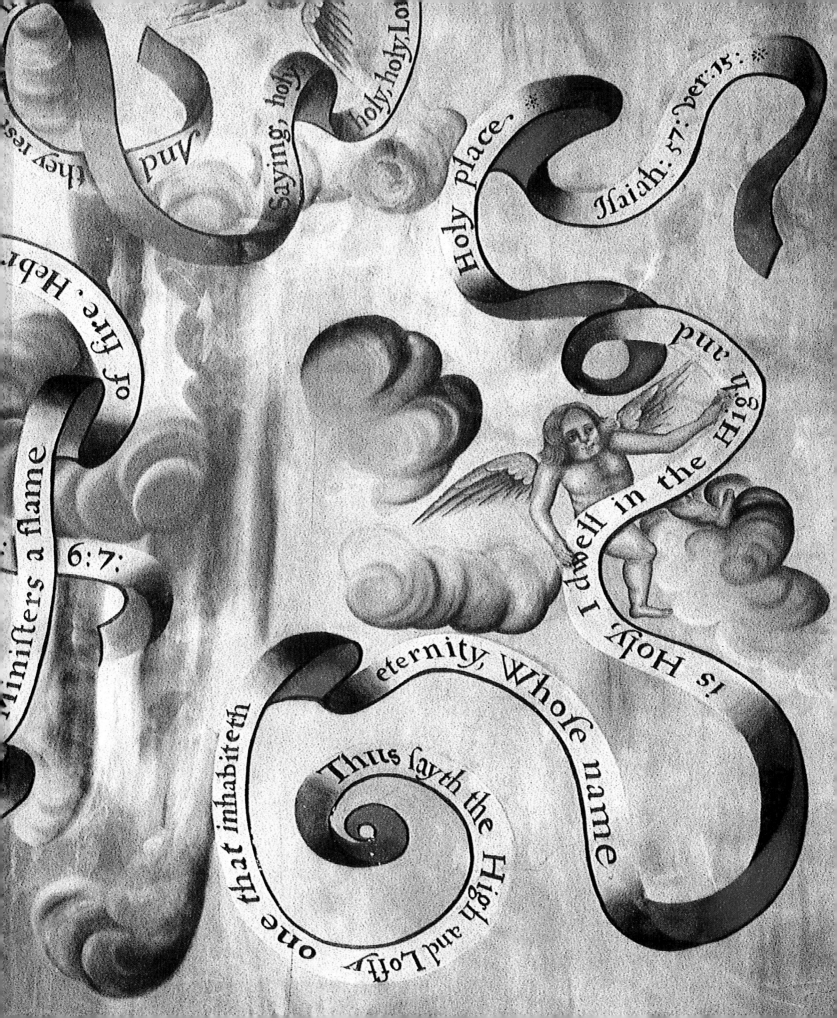